HOW MANY *Kids*
DO YOU HAVE?

Jamie Murray

"The brutally honest yet incredibly inspiring conversation about blended families that our society needs. You'll laugh, cry, and feel understood in a way you didn't know you needed."

Jamie Scrimgeour
Life Coach + Digital Content Creator
Host of *The KICK-ASS Stepmom* Podcast
Creator of The Exclusive Stepmom Community

"How Many Kids Do You Have is an AMAZING read! Jamie's style of writing makes you feel like you are going through the experiences right along with her. Each chapter offered a precise look into what it is truly like for those of us in blended families. She kept us intrigued page after page with her wit; once we started reading, we couldn't put it down until the end! This book is a phenomenal must-read for anyone attempting to blend a family and a perfect illustration of what it is to go through the process of blending families."

April Kirk and Loren Kirk
Hosts of the Co-Parenting Past Chaos podcast

"Jamie Murray's How Many Kids Do You Have? is an incredibly insightful book about blending families and the unique challenges they face. Jamie offers a refreshing and vital perspective on what it means to parent in today's reality where fewer families resemble the traditional 'nuclear family.' Jamie's voice is authentic, heartwarming, and instructive. This book should be read by all parents navigating separation and divorce, and their new partners."

Anita Volikis
Resilience Coach, Lawyer, and Author

"Jamie writes with a profound honesty that only comes from earned and learned experience. She made me laugh out loud, then brought me to tears within a few sentences, making reading her book a wildly engaging human experience.

This isn't about seeing the bright side, blessing the messy, or any other trope designed to bypass the real-deal pain of divorce and starting over, this time with kids in tow. It's a radically transparent account of how HARD it is; Jamie's words and Texan insights hold the space to simply be witnessed in the shared hardship—and in doing so, make it just a little bit easier knowing that while blended-family life can feel isolating, you are definitely not alone in your experience.

The compassionate lens through which this book is written—for parents, ex-partners, and their families and all the children—is a testament to how much deep-healing and self-awareness work Jamie has done with the intention of simply showing up, unlearning, and interrupting the unhealthy patterning she learned as a kid and openly shares.

This is a beautiful bird's eye view on the relationship dynamics of "what it's actually like," including layers of loss, love, forgiveness, and hope, which I highly recommend to anyone at any stage of their own blending. Y'all are going to love this."

Leisse Wilcox

Transformational Mindset + Success Coach

Best-Selling Author of *To Call Myself Beloved*, Podcast Host

First and foremost, to my own blended family: my husband who sees me when I cannot see myself, my oldest for growing with me, my boy teenager for fully accepting me, my girl teenager for inviting me into her world, and my baby girl for helping us balance it all.

And for all the blended families across the world unsure of what they are creating and in need of some enlightenment to get through, may you know you are not alone or any crazier than the rest of us. You are loved; you are your own special blend of love.

AUTHOR'S NOTE

The inherent risk of writing and publishing a book this personal is exposure and vulnerability. My biggest fear is never my own exposure, but that of my loved ones. I have taken great lengths to produce something that did not expose for the sake of exposure but rather to establish a starting point from which the reader can see themselves in my story and start tapping into their own. My primary goal has been to expose myself more than anyone else. I have an enormous amount of love and respect for the stories being shared and for the people they involve. They are my family. Please note: I am not a medical doctor or a counselor. Any advice or opinions offered are solely based on my years of personal experience.

Contents

FOREWORD

Blended families make up a diverse population. We include families of all creeds, genders, marital statuses, socioeconomic statuses, and colors. A blended family means someone in the partnership has a child or children from a previous relationship. Blended families face a specific set of obstacles, not only in making their marriages work but also in creating a family together. And this shit is hard. It doesn't come with an instruction manual or a "how-to" guidebook.

These days, a stepfamily is frequently referred to as a blended family, which I like. The very connotations behind the word "stepfamily" make it feel like, to me, that we are permanently separated from one another, as if the gap between us will never be bridged. The term "blended family," at least, feels like the pieces have come together to create something new—a very personalized puzzle where all pieces fit together, even if some are old and some are newer. It also, however, sets us up for failure. While the term is progressive and inclusive, it grossly overestimates the ease at which our blended families "blend." This very term can sometimes be misconstrued as though the entire process is complete once we initially combine these two homes into one. I personally like the term "blending family." We may never be a "blended family" because that would mean that our journey is finished and the hard work is done. "Blending" is not just a beginning phase when you initially put your two families into one home. It is the ongoing ebb and flow of diverse personalities, behaviors, habits, quirks, and love languages under multiple roofs. We will only ever be a blending family, currently happening, always working on it, no ETA in sight. Blending is our new norm.

Blending means that though there will be moments where we might want to call it quits, we take a moment and listen instead. We approach each other with a bit more compassion, especially when it's hard. We are that much more sensitive and empathetic to everyone involved in our unique blend. It doesn't mean perfect, it just indicates progress and dedication—a dedication to love each other as we are, for who we are, knowing that each come with their own opinion that needs a lot of TLC and delicate handling instead of a quick listen. The modern blending family is the new norm, a norm where maybe, just maybe, everyone involved can coexist and coparent with compassion and openness, where birthdays and holidays can be enjoyed together (with healthy boundaries in place, of course), and where even through conflict and hardship, respect and love can grow and flourish.

INTRODUCTION

Raising kids is the emotional equivalent of having a retirement account. You invest your entire life with hope that at sixty-seven years old, it was all fucking worth it. The sacrifices, the penny pinching, the lost golf games, the missed wine nights, the self-discipline, the planning, the balancing acts. The martyrdom you willingly took part in. The expectation is that sacrificing right now will lead to happiness later. We all enter parenting with the belief that the future that awaits us after all those years of sacrifice will be worth it. But didn't we all know what we were getting into? Didn't we all know how hard it was going to be? Didn't we all get warned? Didn't we expect to make sacrifices? So why are we bitching about it now? Isn't it all worth it in the end? Is it all worth it?

The truth is, yes. We did know. We did get warned. Our culture warned us, our music warned us, our friends warned us, our parents' own lives warned us. "Motherhood is hard . . . parenting is hard . . . kids are a lot of work . . ." (Insert whatever you've been told on this wonderful journey that is parenthood.) We did it anyway, because . . . what's that lie, the one we all tell ourselves in order to make life choices without being permanently paralyzed? Ah, yes . . . "We will be different, that won't be me, my kids won't act like that, our love is better and stronger than any love that ever existed in the whole entire Universe!" At least that's what my husband and I told ourselves when we merged households to create a brand-new family. Seemed easy enough, right? Boy meets girl, boy has two toddlers, girl has one preteen, boy and girl have baby together. Wave the magic wand, say some magic words, and voilà . . . a family! And they all lived happily ever after!

Spoiler alert: It didn't go quite like that. It went more like unrealistic expectations, unresolved insecurities, barely buried contempt, and, sometimes, volatile anger. Boy, we did not see that coming. It's just that no one really knows how hard things can be when a family blends. We tend to believe that love is going to be enough, but it's not. The difficulty of blending two families into one is sorely underestimated. It is an intense and arduous process. Blending children, blending adults, blending histories, blending personalities, blending habits, blending dreams and desires, blending in-laws, blending homes, and blending life goals provides just a glimpse of the totality of blending two families. As our four children grow and get closer to adulthood, our family faces new dynamics and new dilemmas. Still, God willing, my husband and I will get to live out our lives together, side by side, witnessing the beautiful lives each of these four children will create for themselves. I wouldn't give up a moment of the hard stuff if it changed where we are today. Actually, that's a lie. It is really hard. I would definitely give up some of it.

I can proudly say that our children love each other. They consider each other siblings. Not half, not step, but siblings. They are siblings in the sense that these are the people they grew up with and the future adults they will run to when they need to remember where they came from. I have watched the harm siblings can do to each other, and I have witnessed the strength of having strong, nurturing ties between siblings. Because I am an only child, my husband likes to tell me I don't understand how siblings "work." So, as an observer, I must say siblings are either the most important thing to each other or the least. There is nothing in between. We have tried to raise our children with the expectation that our family is real and permanent. We have tried to raise them with the intention that when we are gone, they have each other. Our hope for them is that, as adults someday, they can lean on each other, trust each other, and support each other.

"Forever" is a tricky promise to make in a blended family, but for us, it has been an absolutely necessary one to uphold. There is always the fear that we blend these children, promise them forever, then can't follow through. Blended families break all the time. But so do first families, and no one ever judges two biological parents for promising their children they will be together forever. The promise of a forever family isn't without its danger, but if you can't promise forever while you are in it, you might ask yourself why you are in it. Creating a new family from the ashes of old ones cannot be taken lightly. Kids get hurt when their first family breaks, but if the second family breaks too, far more permanent damage can set in. If every human involved within this newfound familial dynamic has agreed to try again, risk their hearts again to create something new, then a full-on commitment must exist. It is our children's hearts we are playing with, after all. And breaking those hearts is not something any parent ever enjoys doing.

Blended families are changing the landscape of our culture. They are our new norm, and to find success, we must feel safe and cultivate an open perspective to let the dirty details out. We are not alone, but we are living in the shadows. Our schools, our doctors, our extended families, and even our friends are still ill-equipped to handle us. Admittedly, we are a lot to handle. We have beautiful days followed almost immediately by emotional outbursts and meltdowns straight out of a civil war. When people say, "I don't know how you do it," they are correct. They literally have no idea how we do it and how we keep doing it without going batshit crazy.

In a blended family, you aren't just blending furniture and dishes. You are blending multiple personalities, behaviors, and quirks as well as heartache, despair, grudges, hurt, and resentment. Although—total sidenote here— unpacking your husband's half of his ex-wife's set of dishes can be reason for an emotional breakdown. All this is to say that in a blended family, you are essentially taking on the energetic and emotional imprints that you each come with from your past relationships and first families as well as every other emotionally damaged piece of each human being involved. A blended family is a group of broken people with their own specific history of hurt. We didn't get to be a blended family with no baggage. A troubled past is literally the only reason our new family exists.

Which brings me to the title of this book, *How Many Kids Do You Have?* Seems like a simple enough question. Most people don't think twice about how to answer unless they are in a blended family. Then, the dynamics of how to answer cause their entire life to be on display almost immediately after introducing themself to someone they just met. Nothing is simple in a blended family, especially a question like "How many kids do you have?" The conversation goes something like this:

Every Person You Ever Meet: Blah, blah, blah, small talk, small talk, small talk . . . How many kids do you have?

Me: Four.

Every Person You Ever Meet: Oh, wow, that's a lot of kids. Where do they go to school?

Me: (naming all the schools that fall in different districts)

Every Person You Ever Meet: (looking perplexed) Why do they all go to different schools?

Me: We are a blended family. I had the oldest, my husband had the two middle, and we had the baby together.

Every Person You Ever Meet: How old are they?

Me: Twenty-two, fourteen, twelve, and eight.

Every Person You Ever Meet: Oh, is the twenty-two-year-old your husband's?

Me: (growing agitated because I know this script, and I already answered that question) No, the oldest is mine.

Every Person You Ever Meet: Nooooooo, you are too young to have a twenty-two-year-old. How old were you when you had him?

Me: Seventeen.

Every Person You Ever Meet: Is his father around?

Me: (indignant glare growing as the questions get more personal) No, he only met him a handful of times, and he hasn't seen him since he was four.

Every Person You Ever Meet: Oh my. And what about your husband's children? Do y'all get to see them much?

Me: Yes, my husband shares joint custody with his ex-wife, and we have his son full time.

Every Person You Ever Meet: But why do they all go to different schools?

Me: The two middle children go to schools in their mother's school district, and our daughter goes to a school in our school district.

Every Person You Ever Meet: Oh, I see. But do you get to see them often?

Me: (really fucking irritated now) My husband shares joint custody of his daughter, and we have his son full time now.

Every Person You Ever Meet: So why doesn't he just change schools then?

Me: He doesn't want to and it's only fifteen minutes down the road.

Every Person You Ever Meet: Where does their mother live?

Me: In town.

Every Person You Ever Meet: Do you all get along with her?

Me: It's been ten years now. We have all grown up and learned to accept each other.

My guess is that you're probably finding yourself irritated as you read through that dialogue. Friends, it is quite literally my every day whenever I am out and about or meeting someone for the first time. This conversation usually goes on for about six more increasingly invasive questions before the interrogator realizes just how much they now know about a complete stranger. I finally get tired of putting my life on display, and they finally realize they just asked me to sum up the last two and a half decades of my life in an introduction. I then excuse myself before I'm expected to explain what my shit looked like that morning.

In a blended family, the question of how many kids you have does not have a simple answer. Much like every other aspect of our lives, the layers of complication begin the second we are expected to explain our family. I have never been one to use the term "stepchildren," but for simplicity's sake, I will here. I have raised my stepchildren since they were three and four years old (Irish twins). They are my daughter's siblings and my son's family. I have been present for every meet-the-teacher night, every first day of school, and tens of thousands of practices, sporting events, joys, and sorrows. I show up daily in this world for four children. It has never felt natural for me to answer "two" when someone asks me how many kids I have.

The flip side is that I am not their mother; they have a mother, and I did not give birth to them. One could reasonably argue then that I don't have the right to claim them as my own without qualifying that they are my stepchildren. Like it or not, I choose to claim them as my own whenever given the opportunity. That's the thing about a blended family—there are no right answers, and we are all just making this shit up as we go. I won't judge you for how you answer, so don't judge me for how I answer when strangers ask, "How many kids do you have?"

This book is a love letter to my family and yours. My hope is that by getting real, cleaning out the closet, and beginning an honest dialogue about how blended families function and operate, we might also heal and get stronger together. The world's future depends on blended families being seen, understood, and supported. We must go all in for our marriages and the children our marriages involve. We must talk about how hard everything is so that we can grow, heal, and lead our families the way they need and the way we desire. These kids need their blended families to work in order to grow into stable and productive parts of society. The children involved in blended families today will be leading our world tomorrow. They deserve to feel loved and wanted. They deserve a family. So do we.

I hope that as you read about the inadequacies, epic fails, and debacles of our family's journey, you believe that your family is not all that different. Each failure, every parenting-gone-wrong moment, each and every time walking away seems like a viable option, I hope you remember that this journey we have chosen is not an easy one. It is not easy for the adults or children. But we have chosen it, and there is beauty unlike any other if we can see past the dark moments to create the family we all deserve.

This book is a speaking part in the play of blended families everywhere. It is just one story, from one perspective. The purpose is to open a dialogue about a situation so many of us are maneuvering yet so few are talking about. This book is not a how-to guide, an advice book, or a handbook with seven easy steps to blended-family success. Much like my family, this book is a work in progress. By the time this book is released, my family may be in the throes of our next civil war. I do not have the answers you are looking for. Hell, I don't have the answers I am looking for. This book is one account of one family in hopes it makes us all feel a little less crazy and alone. So, buckle up, buttercup; it's going to be a bumpy ride!

Current statistics state that while approximately half of first marriages end in divorce in the United States, a staggering 75 percent of blended marriages do.[1] What we are doing isn't easy, and the world hasn't really acknowledged all the challenges modern blended families continue to face. The focus tends to be on helping the nuclear family stay together, minimizing divorce at all costs, and preserving the family structure. But what if that no longer works? What happens when that structure starts crumbling because of abuse, toxic behavior, or simply genuinely misaligned people who have tried everything from counseling to therapy and everything in between? What happens when two people realize that they are much better parents separately than together? The cold, hard truth is that sometimes people don't need to stay together, sometimes families break apart, and sometimes having a second chance to create the family you desire is exactly what you need. The sad truth is that sometimes people get left, or there just wasn't anyone else around to begin with. If we are lucky enough, we get to try again. We get another opportunity to create the family we want while still honoring the family we had. It is time the world starts valuing what blended families give back to communities. We need the blended families in our communities to be successful. We need to better understand a blended-family culture. We need to clearly define the difference between a blended family and a broken one.

Perhaps the most unique characteristic of blended families is that they do not begin the day a person meets their significant other. Our family origin stories begin years, if not decades, before setting eyes on a new partner's face. Our family stories begin the day children are born to previous partners, in former lives, with distant versions of ourselves. In a blended family, one is simultaneously managing their past, present, and future. They aren't standing at the altar and promising to love, honor, and cherish from this point forward. Oh, hell no. They are standing there in front of God and everyone, promising to love, honor, and cherish this person's entire history. Timelines look different because family dynamics were determined before the new family even existed.

Don't agree? Take a moment and reflect on these questions: Is your life being dictated by a divorce decree? Do you deal with baby-mama (or baby-daddy) drama? Do you fight about stepchildren? Do you defend your biological kids? Do you argue about who pays for what, or how often you get to see your children, or which holidays you get to spend with them? Do you feel like your head might explode from the weight of it all? Uh-huh. Your family started years before you met your new partner. We are blended families because we fell in love with someone who already has children with a former partner, and sometimes those people still exist here in the present. And generally, most of them aren't going away in the future. That's a lot for any person to take on.

When we meet our significant other and fall madly in love, we tend to brush aside the challenges this specific love will encounter and the extremely delicate care it is going to require. We let love blind us to the logistics of what is truly needed to blend two families into one in a functional and healthy way. Spoiler alert: You can't. The perfect blended family won't happen, no matter how hard you try, because it doesn't exist.

When a couple first meets each other, there is always some sort of a façade involved. For instance, when I went for weekend visits to see my new boyfriend, I'd down a half a box of Gas-X because I was terrified that I'd let one rip at an inopportune moment. Dating is fake. Everyone wants their new partner to see them in a certain light, so they aren't always honest in their representation to one another. In our early stages of dating each other, my husband gave me the impression that he and his ex-wife were on great terms. She would call, I would hear conversations between them and the children, and all seemed well. He never spoke an ugly word about her, which I found both comforting and threatening. *Like, if they get along so fucking well, why aren't they still married?* Unbeknownst to me, they viscerally hated each other (which made me oddly more comfortable). They went through a tough divorce, and she had no idea her young children were sometimes spending weekends at my house, which was an hour and a half away from her. My husband also said that he had been divorced for more than a year because he didn't want to scare me away by telling me that he had only been legally divorced for three months when we met. While this detail would have been important in helping me understand their dynamics, dating is fake, and we all embellish to some degree, especially when you come across *that* person—that one who, for reasons you cannot explain, you can't walk away from. When *that* one shows up, you tell them whatever it takes just to have one more conversation with them.

When we transition from strangers to giddy-headed lovers to insta-family, we may not be whole and healthy individuals. We may not yet be at peace with our own past or be ready to begin again. While we may *want* to be ready to move forward with our lives, our souls may still be healing. The reality that we are often bruised and broken people moving forward in no way diminishes the love and significance of our blended family. It is just one more layer to an already overly complicated way of being. If anything, our brokenness just further illustrates how important this new family will be to every single member involved. There are aspects of ourselves we may not even be able to work out until we have the person we want to spend our life with by our side. Some healing doesn't begin until then, so we can't expect that healing process to be complete when we meet. In our particular blend, our love exposed pieces of ourselves that could only be coaxed out by each other. We came face-to-face with certain parts of our hearts—our vulnerability all out in the open—something that could only occur with the help of our current partner. We have all grown in ways we could only have done together as this family.

Children's well-being is just as dependent on these blended families. After loss and heartache, they need to know love can still exist. That family doesn't look one certain way. That family will not abandon them just because two individuals had to go their separate ways. That they are still loved because they were birthed from love, of love, with love—which means love is the tie that binds and seals souls together even through the distance, the trials, and the strife that comes our way. Our children need to see us work through our loss to find happiness again because there's a fifty-fifty chance that they end up in their own blended family one day.

Our blended families hold the opportunity to create resilient, hopeful, and empathetic adults who move through life with conscious intention in every relationship—romantic or otherwise. To be honest, a large portion of future adults will come from blended families. If we do not begin creating language for them to articulate their own backgrounds and stories, we will have half a generation of emotionally stunted adults leading our world. Every child in a blended family is affected. Our families deserve a place in the world to be valued and understood.

...

"Change" can be an expletive in a blended family. It's true that change is the only constant we have because our families are in constant states of ebb and flow. We are always growing, evolving, changing. When my husband and I first met, we had two toddlers and a preteen. Today, we are parents to a grown young man, two teenagers, and an eight-year-old. Our family dynamics change as our children age, and as we age. Additionally, our dynamics change when extended families change. In a blended home, our families are regularly hurdled into change, often not even by our own choices. Biological parents introduce new people, get married, and some of those people may even come and go. When any parent involved dates someone who does not mesh well with the children, that bleeds over into your home. When an absent parent resurfaces, that changes the dynamics in your household. When a baby is added to the mix, the family dynamics at all the homes involved are affected. It's a domino effect. Our homes can become a topsy-turvy hell in an instant. Adjustments in a blended family are our only constant. For instance, my husband and I have yet to even experience our grandchildren, step-grandchildren, marriages, divorces, and all the problems grown children bring to a blended family. While all families experience change, not all families do it with the added burden of ex-partners, previous in-laws, and step-extended families. None of it is easy.

When blended families go through change, bear in mind that change is the trigger your family is rooted in. For our blended cohorts, change will always be scary. Be it positive or negative, it is still just more change. The family dynamics you entered when you started this family will not remain the same. If adults cannot handle the change that they've created for themselves, what the hell do you expect your children to do with it all? In a blended family, no matter how perfect, the children have all experienced trauma to get where they are today, and that trauma started with change.

I remember my son begging and pleading for a family when he was younger. He wanted the whole package: a father, siblings, and a family to call his own. When he and his future stepbrother met for the first time, they took off, wrestling and playing like two puppies in a dog park. As for me and my now-husband, in that moment, as new lovers building a blended life together, we looked at each other with the smugness only a new love can carry. *This is easy. Our love and soul connection will radiate into our children, and they will grow up together in a perfect home filled with nothing but love, unicorns, and rainbows.* We were fucking idiots.

To be fair, I do believe our children have grown up in a loving, healthy, and well-balanced home. It just doesn't look like anything we thought those words would mean. We confused loving, healthy, and well-balanced with nuclear perfection, drama-free, and consistent. It's likely that your version of loving, healthy, and well-balanced won't fit on a Hallmark card and can't be tied up with a ribbon of perfection or bandaged with new toys, shopping sprees, or bonus allowances to buy whatever one's heart desires. Our version of loving, healthy, and well-balanced looks like chaos, hurt feelings, resentment, and the ever-present jealousy. From children on up to the adults, we haven't always given each other our best. The way that blended families create loving, healthy, and well-balanced homes is found in empathy, apologies, and fresh starts. And ours is no different.

In a blended family, your children may accidentally find out the term you used in your phone for your ex because Siri can't follow instructions to permanently delete an old name. In a blended family, a new stepmom may have to apologize to your six-year-old for talking shit about a little girl's mother in front of her. In a blended family, a new stepparent may have to teach a biological child the need to have empathy for her siblings on transition day. In a blended family, a new stepdad may have to face your partner and all your crying children after a massive blowup over parenting because you and your spouse just had a screaming match over the double standards in your home.

If we are being real, these types of situations happen in our loving, healthy, and well-balanced homes more times than any of us would like to admit. We are humans with feelings and emotions—all of which are valid. We aren't perfect. Remember, we did not start our family the day we met our partners. The current dynamics in our family started long before we even entered the picture, which is why so much of what we do is so hard. But don't throw the baby out with the bath water. Don't disregard all the good things with the challenging. Our blended families are not broken homes because of one (or all) of these kinds of scenarios. The beauty of a blended family is that we have a unique opportunity to teach and show our children how real forgiveness looks, how real empathy looks, and how real commitment looks. Our children, biological or step, are growing up in homes where the expectation is divorce, separation, or exile, especially if a marriage, for whatever reason, doesn't work out the way once envisioned. As leaders of these families, we have a golden opportunity to take our flaws and make them examples of grace, love, and forgiveness.

Blended-family goals should not include avoiding conflict but rather embracing it. Conflict is something we face daily, sometimes even hourly. It's what we do before, during, and after the tough moments that make our families loving, healthy, and well-balanced ones. We can't avoid the ugly parts of our stories; our success is based on how we handle those ugly parts. Do we hold our stepchild close when given the chance and say I'm sorry for overstepping my boundaries, or I'm sorry for saying something that wasn't kind, or I'm sorry that today is a transition day and I know how hard that must be on you? Do we hold our biological child and say I'm sorry you haven't had a lot of say in your life, or I'm sorry I couldn't change that reality for you, or I'm sorry change is such a constant in your life that you sometimes question your surroundings? Our blended success doesn't depend on us not fighting or even on a lack of conflict. Our blended-family success depends on us rewriting the script that causes our children to believe in loss and decay. Our success depends on showing our children (no matter how they came to us) that they are loved and won't be left behind or alone.

Our families get to teach commitment and love in a unique way. For us, it is all choice, not obligation. As parents of our blend, we wake up every single day and decide to do it all over again. We chose to love these children. We chose to support our partner's growth. We chose to be a better example today than we were yesterday. Creating a strong blended family isn't like running a 5K. Hell, we aren't even a marathon. Our families are the emotional equivalent of a six-month trek across two continents, barefoot. We aren't in this for the short haul, and we won't see the fruits of our labor for years, if not decades. There's even a chance we won't see any at all. Now, if that doesn't foster loving, healthy, and well-balanced, I don't know what the hell can.

THE BLENDED MANIFESTO

It is up to each of us to accept that we are not just like every other family. Our family dynamics are intense and rooted in heartbreak. That does not mean the world needs our blended families to succeed any less.

CHAPTER 2

Delusions of Grandeur

(How hard it is to make it to your first wedding anniversary)

It's a tale as old as time. Girl meets boy. Boy meets girl. They fall madly in love with each other . . . and all the extra baggage they each bring with them into the mix. Girl and boy decide to spend the rest of their lives together in dysfunctional bliss (or at least that was my fairy tale). If statistics are true, that is how the fairy tale plays out for about half of us. In all honesty, my fairy tale was something more like single, stressed-out, control-freak mom meets newly divorced, not-yet-reformed bad-boy dad with two kids. We met in a bar where I was with my best friends, day drunk and in a rare I-don't-give-a-fuck mood. He approached me, engaged me with the sexiest voice I'd ever heard, and my heart basically stopped right then and there. I partied with Sexy Voice into the night, and neither one of us ever revealed we had kids. How many kids did we have that night? Zero. Nope, my now-husband and I literally did not mention that we had children on the night we met, or during the next few days of text messages, or during the handful of phone calls before our first official date.

Seven days after the night in the bar, following multiple phone and text conversations, I met him at Bubba's Burger Joint on Hwy 281, halfway between our small Texas towns. My knees buckled when I saw him. He was wearing square-toed work boots with old jeans that fell just right over them, a worn-out long-sleeved Gov't Mule T-shirt, and a worn-in baseball cap. Like the really good kind of cap that isn't there because there's an ugly face underneath it. It was the sexy kind of baseball cap that hung just at the eyes, framing his face like a halo. He had the grungy-sexy-disheveled-construction-worker look down pat. He was not only better looking than I remembered, but he remembered what beer I drank and had it on ice, ready for me when I walked in. I mean, come on . . . what's a neurotic, paranoid, lonely girl to do?

I'll tell you what I did: I sat down and said, "There's something I need to tell you. I have a twelve-year-old." I figured I might as well just shit on that farce of a parade right then before we wasted a lot of time and energy just to end up walking away. In grand Jamie fashion, I knew I could scare this handsomely unrealistic mirage-of-a-man away before he could get my panties in a wad. Shit, I'd be home in time for *Sex and the City.* Why live love when you can watch the fictionalized version of it on TV? He just chuckled coyly and said, "I have four kids from three baby mamas." Long pause. Laughter. "Just kidding. But I do have two toddlers with my ex-wife." Hot and funny. *Seriously, WTF just happened?*

There were many "WTF is happening?" moments when we first met at the bar. We stumbled upon each other in an utterly coincidental way. Only it wasn't coincidence. I would have told anyone that love at first sight was about the lamest, most desperate attempt out there to give yourself consent for bad choices. The truth is, though, that we didn't make any bad choices the night we met. And that is quite a feat for two individuals who can conjure up some bad-choice-making vibes. We certainly made out on the dance floor, took too many shots, and felt a whole lot cooler than we probably looked. But we were just, sort of, entranced by each other. We laughed our asses off with some of our closest confidants, swapped embarrassing stories, watched his brother's band play, and were present in the moment, something I had never seen value in before meeting him. It's as if the world slowed down a bit that night, so I did not miss what was right in front of me. To this day, even as I write these words, he still has this effect on me—he brings my world to a complete standstill so that I can be present in it.

The night we met felt like a chance encounter that the Universe had personally lined up for us, probably because we are so stupid that if left to our own devices, we would have messed it all up. For starters, I was not supposed to be out that night. My son had pulled some preteen bullshit a few weeks before, and he was serving a four-week sentence at home. And as every single mother in the world knows, when you ground your children, you are grounding yourself. So, I was on track to spend my final weekend as prison guard, stuck at home, when a babysitter literally pulled up and knocked on my front door. My son's best friend and his dad showed up to take him camping. The dad explained that they had been out and had forgotten his phone, so they just thought they'd stop by to invite my son. While I am in no way condoning early release for good behavior, what kind of mom denies a young boy a camping trip? *Yes. Yes. You can take him. Now. Go get packed, kid.*

Thus, I was out with my best friend in the world, the one who would become my maid of honor, the one I ran to when I accidentally hung up on my now-husband the first time I ever called him because I had no idea what to say. She told me to call him back because "We like this one, Jamie, we like him." She was right. *We did like this one. A lot.*

...

Seven months later, our family was born. We moved quickly, but that's how it goes sometimes when you've been there, done that. We were thirty and thirty-four years old, so this wasn't our first rodeo. Given the path of destruction behind each of us, we had pretty much figured out what we wanted for the next time around. Seven months of courtship is not the right path for all, but in our world, it felt right. I had raised my son completely on my own since the day he was born, and my now-husband's lifelong goal of becoming a father had already come true, it just happened to be with a woman he was incompatible with. They were married just long enough to produce Irish twins, and by the time we crossed paths, we were both intentionally single with no desire for anything otherwise.

When my son was born, I had no doubt I would grow up a little, fall in love, and have the family I always knew I deserved. When that did not happen year after year, I felt like I had failed in some way. I had done the hoping, the waiting, the dating the wrong ones, the not-wanting-to-go-through-life-alone. For twelve years I had willed the power of a real and good love to find me, to grow my family, to give my son a father, to give me more children, to give me someone with whom I could share my life.

After all that time, I had just started to like myself, maybe for the first time ever. I had finally accepted that I needed to make my life permanent instead of waiting for something "more." And that's when *he* walked in, and not a moment too soon. Perhaps the Universe had been waiting for me to figure out how to make myself happy so that it could finally send me on my next journey.

My husband and I both come from broken homes and broken childhoods. In our blend of six, our family dynamics are a direct result of everything we had been through as people before we met, including absentee parents, difficult divorces, abusive family members, and family members suffering from mental illness. In our blended family, we are all survivors.

When we moved in together and started our family, we were both unsure about marriage. We truly gave little effort to the planning of what this new life *would, should,* and *could* look like for everyone involved. We were high on love and staggeringly disillusioned. I think this disillusionment may be the case for a lot of blended families because it's all so overwhelming, and if you ever gave any real thought and planning to the *woulds, coulds*, and *shoulds*, you'd never fucking do it. By the time we moved in together, I had a thirteen-year-old, he had a three-year-old and a five-year-old, and we knew we wanted to have a baby together. We did not want to continue dating long distance, dragging our children to each other's homes for weekend visits, and missing the mundane yet magical moments of life with each other—not if we didn't have to, and we didn't have to. I rented out my house, commuted an hour and a half each way, and we started a family. My husband's favorite phrase is "Sometimes you just gotta put your balls on the line," and so we did.

I remember the look of horror on my mother's face when she came for her first visit after our blend had officially been created. I literally had children hanging off the backs of couches, jumping across our still-unpacked living room, and carrying cardboard lightsabers. Her grandson was leading the pack, and the two little ones were squealing in delight while chasing after their "big brother." My son and I had gone from a home of two, filled with quiet evenings and easy mornings, to a family of five and absolute chaos. But that first year of our blended life, though utterly chaotic and filled with upheaval, had many completely beautiful moments that gave us a glimpse of the family we could become together. On our first blended Christmas, for example, we got every family member a Nerf gun and enough "bullets" to take out a small army. For years following, we lived in a never-ending game of "Nerf Wars." No one was safe, and you never knew when or where the ambush would happen: the children attacking the parents, the boys ambushing the girls, the girls hiding in the dirty laundry pile, the parents coordinating sneak attacks. We had fun—the laugh-until-your-belly-hurts-and-fall-to-the-ground kinda fun. And fun was something I had never been entirely comfortable having before.

...

Like most new families, we didn't have balance when our blend first blended. We didn't know when to talk things out versus when to walk away. Quite frankly, we barely knew each other. We hadn't yet learned what makes the other tick or just flip their shit. We didn't understand each other's ebbs and flows. In most relationships it takes years to uncover these things, but in a blended family you are discovering and learning about each other with umpteen little eyes watching your every move from day one. We didn't get to enjoy quiet weekends together making love, sleeping in, or peacefully sipping coffee like new couples without twenty-seven children get to do. We started on day one with three children—three active and involved children, all with their own respective schedules. Our dating life looked more like the Mayhem commercials than Club Med. My husband had two young children 50 percent of the time, and I had my son 100 percent of the time. We spent the first three months of our relationship sneaking my husband in my house after my son went to bed and sneaking him back out before he woke up. Even then, it was only on the days he didn't have his kids.

Dating and getting to know someone looks quite different when you already have children. There is no lead-in. You meet, you love, you have a family. It's that quick. Of course, you can take it slowly and wait for the rare occasions when neither of you have your children, but I didn't have an extended family who could help me out, so finding a babysitter was something like an act of congress. Thus, we decided to introduce our kids relatively soon into our dating relationship. We decided to rip off the bandage and see how it went. Given that our feelings for each other were growing so strongly, so quickly, we didn't really want to get much further down the road only to realize that our blend didn't stand a chance of success. For us, there wasn't much point in pursuing a relationship if there was no possibility of a happy and cohesive family in there as well.

Dating with children often means you miss out on the privilege of really getting to understand how one another "works." You don't get the time to simply enjoy each other. You don't get to sit next to your boyfriend in a restaurant, but you do get to regularly hear about how pretty his ex-wife is because his children love to talk about their mommy. You get to steal hugs in the hallway because you're trying to give your children the space they need to accept this new relationship, and you often don't get the luxury of time to figure out what your marriage will look like. It's balls to the wall, out of the gate. You are either all in, or you're not. We were all in, and that meant sporting events, school schedules, and playdates from day one.

In our first year of dating, we spent a total of one weekend alone together. My then-boyfriend planned a beach trip for us, and we finally got to lie around naked all weekend long, just drinking, talking, and making love. I felt like Cinderella before the condom broke. I still remember that weekend like it was yesterday. I also remember his children crying on the phone because he was missing a T-ball game to be with me. *Have I mentioned how tough the dynamics are in a blended family?*

...

When we first began talking about moving in together, marriage was off the table for us both. He had just had a heavy dose of how badly a marriage can end, and I had personally never seen a marriage work. Period. We both believed we could commit to one another and begin a family without the noose of a marriage. We even planned my pregnancy around my teaching schedule, but not an ask for marriage. I'm still not exactly sure when we changed our thinking. At some point, it just became clear that we weren't *avoiding* marriage, we were *missing out* on it. We didn't dwell on it, and we barely talked about it, but as the family grew, something shifted.

On our first Christmas morning as a family, my son and then-boyfriend disappeared into the other room. They emerged side by side, and in front of all three children, my now-husband presented me with a small box with a ring, and we promised to stick it out... until death do we part, motherfucker. We were married ten months later in the same Irish bar where we first met.

Marriage did not create our commitment to each other, or our family, but it did solidify it. We had been living together, had a mortgage together, and one would assume marriage wouldn't be all that different. One would be wrong. Very, very wrong. Marriage somehow still changed things. We stood in front of our children, our family, and our friends and promised "our forever" aloud for all to hear—and to grow our own blended family every single day, hot or cold, happy or sad, light or dark, and this promise meant that we could not walk away easily. Some days that would be the only thing I had.

...

Many of our family-folklore favorites took place that first year. A fan favorite in our house is commonly referred to as the "Crunchy Taco Incident." Structure had yet to exist in our new life. Being a newly divorced father, my husband was a bit lackadaisical for my style. My new stepchildren were adjusting to a stepmother coming in and changing things, and we found ourselves in a particularly difficult season of "I hate you, and I won't eat what you cook for me."

So, six months pregnant and barely hanging on, I listened as the five-year-old dared tell me that the tacos tasted nasty. Just like that, I flipped my shit on everyone at that table. Moms, you know how this goes: "I am so sick of this crap. I am tired of this picky-eating bullshit. It's so rude. I make the time to make sure we have dinner on the table. It's freaking crunchy tacos, for Christ's sake." Two little faces exchanged scared looks with each other and then, heads down, they tried to eat their crunchy tacos. My husband bravely spoke up first. "Uh, honey, you might want to taste these tacos. I don't think it's your cooking, but I do think something is wrong with them." As I pushed my breath down into my gut, I bit down, and sure as fuck, I had managed to pick up a box of crunchy taco shells that could only be described as having plastic baked into them. I don't know if that box had just gone stale after sitting on the shelf of our one-horse-town grocery store for five years, or if it was part of a whole batch skipping past quality control, but those shells were anything but edible. Mouth full and trying to chew my food, I surrendered. I had flipped out, and now I sat there looking like the ass I was. And no one could keep from laughing. We laughed until we hurt, then we went out for tacos.

I also surrendered in other ways that day. I looked at those two beautifully fragile little faces, and I remembered that they were going through some shit too. Their world had been turned upside down just as much as everyone else's, only they had the least amount of say in any of it. They couldn't even read or write yet, let alone communicate a feeling. They didn't hate me, they didn't even hate my cooking. It was just the only thing they could control in what must have felt like a terribly out-of-control life to them. And I'd like to say that from this point forward I learned to pay attention to their needs, to not take their actions personally, and to never let their actions make an impact on my marriage. I'd like to say that, but I'd be lying. It would be many more years before I truly had empathy for the life my two stepchildren had to live, constantly being stuck between two worlds. It must be really difficult to pack up your things every seven days and leave your creature comforts in one home only to try and readjust in another home, every week until you are eighteen years old.

Since that night, whenever we have crunchy tacos, I get lovingly harassed. "Remember when you made those nasty tacos and yelled at everyone when you didn't believe they were bad?" they love to remind me. It's one of our earliest shared memories. Our children can remember the house, the kitchen, and the table we were all sitting around. For years, every time I'd get roasted about the Crunchy Taco Incident, I'd think, *Jesus, let it go already. I made bad tacos one time and didn't believe you because I was losing my shit trying to make it all work.* Their teasing used to bother me because it was a reminder of the part of me that had not yet created empathy for my stepchildren, and it embarrassed me because it represented parts of myself that I didn't like. I wasn't always nice to them, nor did I always have the patience they needed. I hadn't yet learned how to love them.

People assume that falling in love with someone's children is as easy as falling in love with your new partner. It isn't. I had love for them immediately, and I would have gone all "mama bear" in a heartbeat if need be. But to have the gleam in your eye when your kids walk through the door, the flush of love you feel all over when you see their faces, *that* takes time in a blended family. It takes time, forgiveness, humility, and grace. I have those things now in a way I didn't back in the beginning. I recently dropped my stepson off at high school for the first time, and as I watched him walk across the parking lot, all I could see was that chubby four-year-old I met a decade ago. My heart felt that flush of love and pride that parents know so well. Until you have created the history of your family, you can't expect to feel like one. And that's okay.

As I grew as a person, and as a stepmother, the Crunchy Taco Incident became a fond memory I now treasure. It is this shared history that has bonded us together and made us a whole unit, and when a memory like this one is shared with one another, it shifts from debacle to family legacy in no time at all.

THE BLENDED MANIFESTO

Blending a new family is hard, especially in the beginning. It's okay to admit you fucked up and then laugh about it together. It's actually crucial to growing as a family.

CHAPTER 3

Meeting Your Future Step-Wife

*(How hard it is to share your future
with someone else's past)*

I met my husband's ex-wife for the first time on a T-ball field eleven years ago. It did not go well. The story has become well-known folklore within our small circle of friends. "Remember the day you and the ex-wife met each other for the first time out at the T-ball fields?" is a crowd-pleasing question for sure, primarily because our two houses hated each other for so many years, and from day one, our small town got a front-row seat to the shit show that was our lives. The relationship between the two houses did not improve for many moons. Like eight years of them.

At the time of my first meeting with the ex, my then-boyfriend and I were spending most weekends together. On the days when he did not have his kids, he would come over to my house, and when he did have his kids, my son and I would usually go to his. The first meeting happened on one such fateful weekend. His son had a game, and my husband was a coach on the team, so they were warming up on the field. I was sitting on the bleachers with his toddler daughter and my son when his daughter said she had to go to the bathroom. I promptly escorted her to the restroom, and as we walked back to the bleachers, a woman with tears streaming down her face came running up to us. It was the ex-wife. She proceeded to grab her daughter, then headed back to the bleachers where she cried to the other mothers from the team about how upsetting it was that she had not been told I would be coming to the game.

My son and I, our belongings still sitting on the bleachers that were now a triage center and having no transportation of our own, timidly avoided eye contact and grabbed our things. We then proceeded to sit in the grass near the outfield by ourselves. A little while later, the ex-wife walked up to me as we sat in exile and continued to cry, and apologize, all while warning me that he would leave me one day just like he left her. I will never forget the fear-stricken look on my son's face that begged the question, *What the fuck are you getting us into, Mom?*

The truth is that I had no idea what I was getting us into yet. I barely knew the details of my husband's divorce, only that according to him, it was behind him. And maybe it was behind him, but it was not behind her. To her credit, my husband is not the most sensitive man in the world. He is flawed. He can be cold. He was not happy, and he was not a good husband to her.

Some husbands have a way of compartmentalizing in a way most wives do not. Just because they can shut off emotionally does not mean unresolved feelings do not resurface and subsequently guide their actions. When unresolved emotion resurfaces, it never comes out in rational, kind, understanding, or calm ways. Instead, it almost always results in ugly behaviors and leads to broken relationships. Unbeknownst to us at the time, we had a lot of unresolved shit to keep us stocked up on hatred for many years to come.

Sometimes, first introductions do not go well in a blended family. One person may have the ability to lock away the past, while another needs more time and healing. Looking back, I wish we had talked about how to meet his ex-wife. I wish we had talked to each other about it, and I wish we had talked to her about it. In a perfect world, it would have been in a private setting after the details had been discussed in advance by all parties involved. Instead, I didn't ask any questions, my husband ignored the situation, and his ex-wife felt blindsided. We were not yet able to think or even consider mutual respect and relationship dynamics and just how important they would be as the years passed. We did not yet value how important our relationship with her would become, or how much of her life would make an impact on our new family. We just had no blueprint for how to maneuver this weird triangle we found ourselves in, which meant we all led reactively instead of responsively—with anger, accusations, hurt, fear, jealousy, and resentments . . . all the heavy hitters. My husband very much felt like he had divorced her, and therefore, she didn't matter anymore. He still struggles to show his ex-wife empathy. Hell, sometimes he still struggles to show me empathy.

...

Over the years, things did not improve much. We were a recipe for disaster: two cups divorced people, one quart new wife, three tablespoons stepchildren, one dash new baby, then some salty, tangy, spicy seasoning to taste with extended family members. Hello, T-ball days! We caused more than one scene, provided our small town with an endless stream of entertainment, and outwardly disrespected each other on the regular. Ain't love grand! And it always seemed that whatever new hatred, jealousy, and resentment we were going through unleashed itself on the impossibly unforgiving dynamics of the T-ball field. Who needs a stage and popcorn when we have the whole field? We had ex in-laws still pissed off about a divorce, new in-laws entering the picture, and old in-laws stuck in between. Loyalty lines after a divorce are tricky little bastards—where to sit, who to talk to, what to say or not say—everyone involved enters a minefield ready to explode with any sudden movement. One can't say too much or too little and certainly can't develop a soft spot for one of the parties. The divide is so large that it seeps into the life of any child involved.

Every year when baseball season rolled around, my chest got tight with anxiety. Similar to those who suffer from seasonal depression, I got seasonal anxiety. My husband has always coached on his son's teams. Every single one of them. So that left me fending for myself, keeping the sharks at bay as I roamed around the fields, not totally sure I even belonged there, my young teenage son, always by my side, never saying out loud what we were both thinking: *WTF are we doing here, Mom?!*

One day I got cornered and scolded by a complete stranger in the field's bathroom. She told me that she had known the kids since they were babies, and they weren't ever going to be mine. Yes, a stranger actually approached me in front of a metal toilet, unsolicited, just to remind me I wasn't important and wasn't ever going to be. As it turned out, my husband and his ex-wife didn't even know this woman to any real extent. For whatever reason, she just felt the need to put me in my place as the new girlfriend. To be clear, I am no homewrecker. My husband was officially divorced when I met him. But to the townsfolk, I was the newcomer, the intruder, the other woman. I don't know about other places, but small-town Texas don't take kindly to new folk, and I was new folk.

As the years went on, life got better, and we all learned to show mutual respect for the sake of the kids involved. Okay, who am I kidding? That's a total crock of shit. For the most part, we did none of those things. We have now grown a lot and learned a lot. In fact, just last weekend we ran into someone from that same small town, and at the baseball fields no less. We reminisced about little league, and we all made a few wise cracks about the good ol' days. Our old friend then complimented the three of us and said it seemed like we were all really getting along well. We smiled, all proud of ourselves, and reflected on the personal growth we have made. We said our good-byes for the day and excitedly looked forward to catching up on day two of the baseball tournament.

A whopping twenty-four hours later, we all returned to the tournament, and before the second game of the day even started, we had emotional breakdowns, tears, parenting fiascos, and another scene right out of the good ol' days. Kids with meltdowns, parents with no idea how to intervene or help, and stepparents trying to save the day. Exactly one day after being complimented about how much we have grown, we had a blended-family scene for the highlight reel, extended family present and all. So truly, while we have grown immensely as a trio of blended parents, some habits are hard to break. Even with growth, some things will always remain the same, unraveling exactly like they always have. Like the old jeans on the top of your closet, you know they won't ever fit you again or serve you well, still you cling to their familiarity.

So, how much has really changed over the last decade? Well, despite the events of that weekend, a lot really. We sit together now, and it is actually easy. It feels effortless. But it took a lot of mutual and conscious effort to get to this place with each other. Seating arrangements in a blended family are not easy. We have done all variations: sitting miles apart and purposely placing visual obstacles in between us because even the sight of the other party turns into red hot rage, sitting within a reasonable distance of each other so that the kids don't feel so torn between which family they visit with, returning to sitting miles apart because the drama going on behind the scenes has hit a particular high that week. Seating also depends on who is present. *Are the grandparents present? Do I say hello? Do they want me to say hello? Should I just mind my own business? Is it rude if I just mind my own business?* And then there are the children who do everything in their power to make the situation exponentially more uncomfortable: *Can my baby sister sit with me and my mom? Come over and meet my baby cousin. Can I show my mom something on your phone? Can you buy me candy? Can my mom buy me candy? My mom needs to know if you picked up the team pictures already*, and so on. T-ball for a blended family can be a ruthlessly painful experience. In fact, making seating arrangements that bode well for your blended family can be a sport in and of itself, one that leaves you feeling like the referee, the offense, and the defense, all at the same time.

The real change isn't in the details though, it's in the dynamics. For example, the feelings that wash over your entire body when you see each other. I think that is what changed the most, which then allowed other things to fall into place a bit more frequently. Ten years ago I could feel the heat come over my body just being around my husband's ex, just having to greet each other or, alternatively, *not* greet each other. I'd feel my skin get warmer, my stomach tighten, and something between anger and fear would cause my jaw to clench. I don't know why I felt anger and fear, but that's what it was. It was that feeling you have when you have no idea how the interaction will go or whether you will be able to manage your own emotions. And then, of course, that feeling you have when you don't know what everyone around you will say about your family.

That weekend the three of us fixed the problems together. Okay, "fixed" may be an overstatement. "Handled" may be more appropriate. We still disagreed, we still saw only our own side of the situation, and we still had meltdowns, but in the end we all walked away with our dignity.

We, our full blended family, has hit really hard times as two of the children become teenagers at the same time. Just as we finished the little kid season of this blended family, we've been launched right into the what-the-hell-do-we-do-with-two-teenagers season. Living arrangements are being altered, children's bodies are changing before our very eyes, and emotions are running high. We cannot stop children from growing up, we cannot avoid the hard parts of adolescence, but our relationship as adults is better today than any of the years before. Please do not confuse *better* with *fixed*. God willing, we have decades more of this weird triangle we live in. If we are only one decade in and seeing change, then imagine what another few could bring. We weren't prepared for what we were getting into, and we may still royally fuck it up most days, but we are all survivors, and we will wake up each day and try again. For us, for our kids, for our new blended family that we have committed to and chosen to love.

...

A good example of where we are today and how our dynamics have evolved happened a couple of months into the quarantine of 2020. Step-wife (as I have come to lovingly call her) came by to pick up the kids. She was getting ready to open a new boutique in another state and had been working her ass off. I poured her a glass of wine, pulled out some leftovers, and a few hours later, my husband and I, our daughter, my stepchildren, and their mother were tearing up the Texas two-step in our kitchen to Pat Green's, "Take Me Out to the Dancehall."

It wasn't always this way. Good Lord, it wasn't always this way. It has been nearly a decade of blending now, and shit still goes sideways. Dynamics are hard, differences remain, resentments exist. I have also shared some of my absolute worst hangovers ever with this woman. Now, I am not condoning the use of alcohol to mask problems, but sometimes getting drunk with someone, crying it out a few times, bonding over splitting headaches the next morning . . . well, it made us human to each other. It made us woman and woman. We saw each other's pain and held space for it, all while still honoring the unresolved emotions that surfaced each time.

When I met my husband, he and his ex weren't but a few months divorced. They had been separated for quite some time, but they had only been legally divorced a few months. He wasn't ready for another relationship, I didn't know shit about being a stepmom, and the step-wife had not yet started her own healing journey. While it does not take a genius to add up these dynamics, the three of us were fucking idiots. We were mean, petty, and when there wasn't a reason to fight between the houses, we made one up.

I'm a know-it-all. A control freak. A recovering control freak and a perfectionist. I had been a single mother for twelve years when my knight in shining armor finally showed up. So, obviously, I was hell-bent on showing how much I knew about raising children, and I was not timid about sharing my unquestionable knowledge. *What time do your kids go to bed?* **I can fix that.** *How many cans of Sprite does your daughter drink in a day?* **I can fix that.** *Why aren't they doing ABCs and math flash cards every night after dinner?* **I can fix that.** It only took me about seven more years to realize that it's actually not my place to fix these things, then about two more years to learn that maybe they didn't need to be "fixed."

My husband was very open about the end of his first marriage. He wasn't happy. Thus, he wasn't a good husband. His account of telling a judge in small-town Texas that he didn't want his children raised with unhappy parents, and the judge dismissing him as a man walking out on a young family is heartbreaking but not uncommon. When we met, neither of us was looking for a marriage. He was newly single. He was showing up for his children during his custody periods as the amazing father that he is, and he was partying his ass off with younger, very attractive "women" (wife air quotes inserted!) the other 50 percent of his time . . . because he could. He was not quite the reformed bad boy I married two years later. Hell, sometimes he still isn't!

Step-wife was carrying her own baggage. The divorce had been hard on her. She thought she was going to raise these children *with* someone and then that story was blown to hell. Sometimes even a bad relationship beats being alone, and with two toddlers, I think that is exactly where she was emotionally. So, when the new-girlfriend-turns-new-wife shows up, all judgy and ready to prove something, shit gets bad.

For the better half of a decade, we played the roles we had been handed—the roles that had already been carved out by society. And we played right into them. Meet the bitchy new wife, the evil ex-husband, and the wronged ex-wife. Add our children to the mix, and voilà! You have an Oscar production on your hands! We were the demented equivalent of the scarecrow, the tinman, and the cowardly lion. Still today, we slip into old patterns, send stupid and mean text messages intended to cause harm, openly question and undermine what the others say and do, and drag our kids in the middle of it all. Our children, all four children involved in our blend, have witnessed the good with the bad. We still screw up. We still get mad. But now we can counter the screw ups and the anger with dance parties in the kitchen.

...

In the beginning of my relationship with the step-wife, if there was a sword to die on, we did. In fact, we have thrown ourselves on so many swords that we still have scar tissue. We have bullied, manipulated, even apologized to each other via text, email, and phone, depending on the current preferred mode of communication. "Passive aggressive" should have our mugshots in the dictionary. We have communicated solely through custody planning apps, group text, and email, then subsequently blocked each other from them all. The pendulum didn't just swing, it made fucking circles.

Some people state that there is no hope for two households to blend, that there is no chance in hell they will ever get along, that hell will freeze over before they look like *The Brady Bunch*. When these claims are made, it is *always* believed to be the other parent's fault. Always. No one has ever said out loud, "Hey, maybe I'm the reason this relationship with the ex doesn't get any better." Ever. But statistics alone would disprove the probability of every person's ex being the leading cause of all the strife in both families.

How is it that people get married to relatively sane people, then end up divorcing a narcissist from hell whose new life mission is to ruin everyone's lives, including their own children's? My friends, behold the power of getting laid. We all understand how love and sex change everything. We start having sex with someone, and everyone else disappears. We refuse to pay attention to the unappealing attributes about that person. We overlook details if they tell a different story than we want to believe. Well, in divorce, this tendency happens in reverse. We would rather see anybody in the world other than the ex. We overlook nothing if it tells the *new* story we want to believe. We don't let anything go. We immediately assume the absolute worst of every intention and interaction. The slightest headshake most certainly means the other parent is secretly seeing a lawyer with a plan to take your child away. Now, I'm not about to say these things don't happen. No doubt they do. Frequently, even. But it seems to me that it always comes back to our inability to look at this other human being, this person with whom we once brought a child into the world, and see anything but all our own hurts and failures. We must be accountable for our part in the unraveling and disintegration of this once head-over-heels union. Time and time again, we are not fighting this other parent, rather the lost life that the other parent represents. If we could overlook our ex's behaviors today, the way we did when we first met, we would find peace.

The kicker of it all is that you do not have to put up with their shit anymore because you are no longer with them. You are gone. Y'all are done. Their insensitivity, their dramatics, their drinking, their gambling, their competitiveness, their complacency—whatever the reason you may no longer be together. None of it is your shit to deal with anymore. You are free. Yes, you can claim it affects you because it affects your children. There are most certainly scenarios you cannot overlook when it puts the safety of your child at risk. Totally understood. But I challenge you to reflect on this question: Is the majority of what you are fighting with an ex-partner about actually endangering your children? The overall answer is no. Are there one-offs? Are there horribly bad parents in the world who do not care for their children in a safe manner? Sadly, yes. But I am confident when I say that they do not make up the majority.

Rather, most of us are looking for reasons to hate each other; we are unwilling to overlook anything about the other person. We cling to resentment, anger, and sorrow like it's our last lifeline. Let a kid get a sunburn or go to school without a lunch? Sit back for World War Fucking 362. Is it shitty when you have a child in pain over a sunburn that could have been prevented? Yes, it is. Does it tug on your heartstrings when your baby goes to school without a lunch and you don't know about it until the end of the day? Yes, it does. Can it be infuriating when Monday morning comes around and you realize you have no jackets at your house because four of them are at the other parent's house? Yes, it is. Still, if we weren't so stuck in our own state of being consumed with "gotchas" and revenge, we could remember that these things happen. And it's okay. Every mistake should not be perceived as the war cry equivalent of Pearl Harbor.

Here's an easy way to look at it: If this were your BFF, that one lifelong best friend who knows all the dirt on you and was present for most of it, if this same scenario happened but it was your dear friend telling you about how they screwed up parenting that day, what would you say to them? Would you damn them to hell, barrage them with every awful thing they have done as a human being in the last ten years, threaten to have their children taken from them, hit them over the head with your judgment of who they should be? No, you just wouldn't. Instead, you would console them, let them know you were concerned about them, listen to them and hold space. You would offer to help in any way you could and empathize. You would understand. What is that you're thinking? Y'all aren't friends? And you don't want to be friends because it's the worst person you've ever met in your life who purposely makes your life awful? Okay, fair enough. I get that. But here's what I didn't get for many years myself: These other adults in your blend are (hopefully) never going away, so laying down the sword is as much for your own sanity as it is for everyone else involved. So, don't be friends. Don't try to know each other. But if the same action you are lamenting over from someone you love would not result in such a hate-filled response, then you shouldn't respond to the ex that way either.

Blended families rarely get it right in the beginning. We don't have guides to navigate us through the least detrimental roads to take. Our stories are not represented because we are often embarrassed about sharing how we have handled situations. We assume everyone else is doing one hundred times better than we are. The truth is, they aren't. Perhaps some are, but I can't say I know of anyone personally. In my experiences, if you get a few blended families together in a room talking, there is always shit happening in someone else's blend as well. And I bet that if you and the other blended families present were asked to toss your problems into a pile in the center of the room, you'd race to take back your problems because they aren't as horrific in comparison. Now, I'm not saying that we should exist on the wagon of "Our family isn't as bad as theirs." Rather, you should start to gain a newfound appreciation for the unique fit that only your blended family has. Also, please don't think that good relationships with an ex do not or cannot exist; it's just not our initial instinct to embrace the former lover with open arms. Every party is guilty of misconducting themselves in a blended family, but it does not mean we don't put our big-girl panties on and try again. Yes, I realize you have already probably tried a countless number of times. Over and over again. But it's okay to try one more time to show empathy, to get to know someone, to forgive inappropriate behaviors, to acknowledge hardships, or to lead with genuine kindness. Quite frankly, it goes both ways, buttercup. Hatred, jealousy, and revenge are hurting you as much as they are hurting everyone around you. At some point, you must accept the history that existed between your spouse and their former spouse. Hate for the sake of hating is not going to create a new family dynamic—one that is built on openness, vulnerability, and respect.

Let me be very clear here. At no point in the last decade did Step-wife and I think to ourselves, "I'm going to forge a friendship with this person." That absolutely never happened. What did happen, however, is that we both got tired of the hatred, the anxiety, the knots in our stomachs, and the physical and emotional turmoil that took place as a result of our mutual hatred. We did not set out to "be friends." We set out to give our nerves a break and to make life a little easier on the children involved.

Today, I am forever grateful to my step-wife for not only sharing her most prized possessions with me, but for growing with me. No matter the number of times we vowed to never speak to each other, never try again, never reach out . . . we always did. One of us always managed to tuck our tail between our legs and try again. My advice to you (if I believed in giving advice) is to truly check your own feelings. It is hard to accept a former partner in your present life, but this blended family triangle is just another dynamic we need to be honest about. Honest enough to say how hard it is, how threatened we may feel, how resentful we are that another woman exists in our home. If we can do that, if we can face our feelings instead of projecting them onto another person, we just might be able to create a real friendship or, at the very least, some mutual respect for each other.

THE BLENDED MANIFESTO

You won't always get it right. You might even hate the ties that still bind. Acknowledge your own resentments about your partner having a previous partner. One that still exists in your world. Allow openness, empathy, forgiveness, and kindness to be your filter. You just might end up learning to respect each other.

CHAPTER 4

Geographical Restrictions

*(How hard it is to have a court order
mandate your life decisions)*

When I met my husband, he was under a court order from his divorce that did not allow anyone of the opposite sex at his home past 9:00 p.m. on the nights he had his kids. Yes, this order is an actual real thing. The argument was that it was not about the other person having sexual relations, it was just about the safety of the children and blah blah blah bullshit. (Apparently, this judge is unaware that gay people exist in the world, but I digress.) When some people get divorced, they are out for revenge. It's a fucking bloody battle. The divorce decree that your blended family is currently relegated to may likely be the product of two people at their worst as human beings, fighting a fight that has no winner. Getting a divorce is one thing but living under the shadow of the decree is another.

I later found out my husband was also under a self-imposed geographical restriction, which he timidly let me know about only after we had decided to move in together. I had naturally started looking for houses halfway between our two towns. Close commutes both ways, right? Wrong. When I started sending him property listings, he finally let me know he had to stay in a specific county range. Like one of them. He had to stay in the same county he was divorced in or he would forfeit his joint custody, reducing his custody from 50 percent of the time to 20 percent, which would amount to not much more than first, third, and fifth weekends. I fell in love with this man in large part because of the father he is. He had given up a lot financially and gone through a contentious divorce, all so that he could raise his kids more than just every other weekend. Not only would I never have expected him to give up any amount of time with his kids, but he wouldn't have done it anyway. And that is the moment I realized dating a divorced man may not be as simple as I had envisioned.

During his divorce, he had worried that his ex-wife might move away so insisted that a geographical restriction be imposed on both of them in addition to his request for joint custody. On everything else he caved, but he would not on these two items. He had been raised by an abusive stepfather in California, while his own father lived many states away. He never had a dad show up to games, pick him up for dinners, or take him to and from school. My husband can be a handful, but he is a present father. He sacrificed a lot to retain the right to be present for every moment of his kids' lives. So, that's when I got to tell my son we were moving an hour and a half away.

This geographical restriction was so binding that when we bought our first home together, we almost didn't get to buy it. We were living in a small rental house at the time, and a short sale came up on a house we could afford. Finding a four-bedroom home on a budget is not a simple task, so we jumped at it, only to find out it was about three feet from the county line, and we were not sure on which side. Ultimately, we discovered it was in the correct county, and we purchased it. Step-wife told me years later that after we bought it, and during a particularly tough season of co-parenting, she drove out to see if it fell on the wrong side of the county line, prepared to move away if so. I could be angry about it, but I'm not. Worse thoughts have crossed my mind over the years. Instead, I felt grateful that the two homes had grown so much that we could be honest with each other. It did not bring up old stuff; I got it. Those were some really tough years we put ourselves through in the beginning.

In the early years, the idea of getting out of that small town crossed everyone's minds. To say it didn't would be a lie. Step-wife worked in a larger town thirty minutes away. She repeatedly approached us with the idea of moving there, or letting her move there with the kids. But my husband said no. I had just moved with my son and had promised him he would finish his courses and graduate at the same school. And while thirty minutes doesn't seem like a big deal, it can add hours to a family's daily routines—school would be thirty minutes away, after-school practices would be thirty minutes away, and so on. I know she felt controlled, and we all felt trapped.

By the time my son graduated, and my husband decided that he could entertain the idea of something his ex-wife wanted, the step-wife was no longer interested in making the move out of our one-horse town. She was dating someone new and looking to change jobs, so she didn't see value in a move anymore. We all spent a few more years there, trapped in our geographical restrictions. It wasn't until all three of us began noticing a decline in the local education system that we once again started talking about a possible move. This time I quickly took control of the situation. I knew if I left the two of them to agree on anything, we'd all be sharing a double room at the local convalescent home in fifty years, still bitching at each other through our dentures about whose fault it was we never left this town.

Eight years and six months later, attorney fees paid and court orders re-filed, the geographical restriction was amended to represent something that was fair and gave us all more control of our own lives. We moved both houses to a lovely hill-country suburb with grocery stores, ample extra-curricular activities, restaurants, and shops. For years we had been forced to run into each other every time we left our homes, every time we went to pick kids up from school, every time we went out to eat, every time we drove through town to the Dollar General, and every time we went to Sonic for a drink. It was just such a small town that there was no escaping each other, ever. My husband and I once took all four kids out for dinner, and we walked in on the step-wife on a date. We were seated two tables away from each other. Throughout the entire dinner, her kids bounced back and forth between tables, showing off their new baby sister to the step-wife's date, and visiting with their mother like nothing in our lives was fucking strange. We must have scared the living shit out of that poor guy; I don't think I ever saw him again. The move out of that town finally gave both homes the space needed to start to live our own lives without the scrutiny of the entire town watching us.

...

Not only does custody paperwork often dictate where and how a blended family can live, it also dictates *when*. For instance, *when* you can take family vacations and *when* you can celebrate holidays. It dictates if you get to see your children on their birthdays and even when dentist appointments can be made or when date nights can be scheduled. When your life is dictated by a custody agreement, you have little control over when things can happen. While I was not present when the custody agreement was created, I was certainly held to the standards of it.

When every holiday rotates by the year, as in our case, a blended family must get creative when celebrating. Rigidity over holiday custody is just straight-up hell. While you can plan and adjust, someone is always left out, which can leave them feeling less loved or wanted. Historically, we would spend holidays at home when my husband had his kids, and we would go see my family when he did not. While it seemed straightforward enough, it was not ever that easy. Only seeing my family when the custody agreement allowed didn't benefit my own children. Leaving his kids out when we spent holidays with my family left my stepchildren feeling unimportant. There is no winning combination, and I don't even have much family to coordinate. I can only imagine the torture for people with larger extended families.

At some point when we had three young children who still believed in

Santa Claus, we just quit traveling for the holidays all together. To be honest, Santa himself is another wrench in the pile of shit that is holiday custody agreements. It's hard enough to keep the farce going for young children in one home. Good effin' luck trying to convince a six-year-old and an eight-year-old that Santa is going to come to two houses just for them because they are so special, and they will get double the presents from Santa because of it. It goes well enough until they go to school where they tell everyone how they got extra presents because they're special, and their little one-home-having-punk-ass friends shit all over their story, so they come home and start asking questions.

In all honesty, holidays were tough those first few years. For many years, actually. We were not yet on good enough terms with the step-wife to be flexible about the time. Neither side was giving up a minute of holiday time, and we all suffered—my stepchildren, my own kids, my husband, his ex-wife. One of them would agree to giving some time on Thanksgiving, or Christmas Day, or Christmas Eve, then the next year one side would remember but the other side would not. We spent days of our holiday breaks in bitter battles, fighting over the desire to just have our family together. The custody dynamics affected our home on every holiday, whether it was our time with the kids or not. If my husband had his children for a holiday, he was over the moon and completely consumed by his two children, almost to the point that it didn't matter if anyone else was around. If he did not have his kids, he was distant and sad and less present. I have never had to share my children, so I cannot understand how hard it must be to routinely miss special moments with them. For me, it just felt like I never fully had him on any holidays.

It took us too many years to put the children before our personal vendettas. It happened gradually, as both homes began to build trust with each other. Eventually, both homes would offer up some holiday time, either a morning or an evening—whatever worked around the custodial parent's holiday plans that year. If we were staying home but the step-wife's family was having a

Christmas dinner, we let her pick up the kids. If the step-wife's family was celebrating on Christmas Eve, we had them for a few hours on Christmas morning. We just started seeing the impact it had on the children. Instead of using custody as a shield to be assholes, we started helping each other have time whenever possible on every holiday. Sometimes it required meeting halfway somewhere or rearranging dinner plans, but all that truly mattered was that my stepchildren got to see both of their parents if possible, and our family got some time when we were all present.

Summer holidays are an entirely different beast. Our summer custody schedule changes dramatically and seems to have been drafted by the town drunk. During the school year, my husband gets school nights as well as weekends, but when school lets out for summer, the extra time during the school week also ends. He gets thirty days of extended summer possession, but it can't be broken up in more than two periods of time, and it must be put in writing before March 1. Step-wife gets one of his regular weekends as her extended summer possession, but it must be selected by April 1. If either parent neglects to make their selection in writing, then extended summer possession selections are forfeited, and my husband automatically gets the month of July if otherwise not selected. Forfeited, like it's a fucking game rather than a child's future or their choice of where they want to spend their time.

You either completely understood what I just explained, or you are thoroughly confused and dumbfounded. This is what custody agreements look like these days. Gone are the days when divorced fathers show up every other weekend and let their kids eat whatever they want and avoid bath times, then promptly return them at 6:00 p.m. on Sunday for the mother to handle the school week. Today, many more fathers are fighting to stay in their children's lives. And it's not just the ex-spouses they are fighting. My husband still breaks down when he describes how he was treated by the small-town judge because he wanted to be involved in the raising of his children. Our courts are just coming around to the idea that a father is as important as a mother, and that fathers need to be present just as much as mothers do. The system has certainly not perfected child-custody agreements, but we are seeing momentum in the fight for children to have the opportunity to know both parents.

One such custody agreement, aimed at offering a biological parent additional time with their children, is the Right of First Refusal. It's a total crock of shit, maybe even more so than trying to keep an adult visitor of the opposite sex out of the home after 9:00 p.m. Right of First Refusal wreaked havoc in our home for years. Step-wife worked in retail, so she worked most weekends. She tried to schedule around the weekends she had the kids, but it often just wasn't possible. My husband hated that his kids got dropped off at his ex's parents' house, or at a friend's house, for eight, ten, or even twelve hours at a time on her weekends. He fought vigorously to enforce the Right of First Refusal in his custody agreement, which stated that if the custodial parent was going to be away from the child for six hours or more, they had to give the other biological parent the right to have the child during those hours. Again, he specifically fought for this right in his custody agreement because of his ex's schedule.

It's a total crock of shit because it is utterly unenforceable. Back in the early years, when jealousy and toxicity ran rampant, his ex-wife never offered up extra time when she had to work. My husband drove himself mad when he knew his kids weren't with her for extended periods during her weekends, and it affected our weekends. It distracted him on the days that we should have had his undivided attention. There were countless numbers of weekends we drove the thirty minutes to her work to see if she was there. We took notes and pictures of her car for the record, and we often got ourselves worked up to the point that my husband pledged to hire an attorney and enforce his Right of First Refusal. Then Monday would roll around and he would realize the futility of it all, but only after it had made an impact on the better part of our weekend.

The flip side is that he never offered it to her either when he had golf tournaments or hunting trips or fishing trips. Those weekends fell straight on my shoulders, and I allowed them to. Maybe I should have demanded that he coordinate such weekend plans with their mother, but I didn't. I thought that I needed to treat his kids just like I would my own. The only thing is that I didn't have another parent to send my kids to, so I never went anywhere without them. It felt petty to tell my husband he could go away for the weekend and then say that I would keep my two children but not his. Honestly, I don't know what was right. A lot of resentment builds up when the stepparent is expected to parent stepchildren for extended periods of time, then be expected to step away from parenting when a biological parent returns. For me, mothering isn't something I can easily turn on and off, which I think is true for most mothers. When children are young, having your stepchildren alone for weekends at a time and not parenting them isn't an option. These days, now that my stepchildren are teenagers, I don't have to "parent" so many of the things that small children require. But back then, it was a heavy load to carry.

On the other hand, those weekends also helped me create a real bond with my stepchildren, and it helped my son connect with his stepsiblings. While that time was emotionally taxing, those were the days when I got to watch my favorite movies with all the kids. Those were the days when I got to create memories with all four children. Those were the days when my stepchildren depended solely on me to take care of them, and those were the days I got to parent everyone as I saw fit without taking another adult into consideration. Talking back . . . nope, not gonna be tolerated. Treating each other badly . . . nope, not okay. Those were the moments I got to teach my morals and values to my children.

Perhaps the same can be said for my husband's ex-wife when she took the kids to her parents' home or let them go to a friend's house to play. My husband didn't agree with her choices, but the bottom line is they were her choices to make. In the same way my husband didn't coordinate his weekends away around her approval, she didn't need to feel obligated to disrupt her routines either. The kids spent time with their grandparents or at friends' houses. They were cared for just the same. My son and I frequently felt like we didn't get my husband's attention when his kids were home, and we didn't get his attention when they weren't. The really hard part is accepting that when you share custody of your kids, you are not in control of them all the time, and you won't get to spend every weekend with them. It can drive you mad but accepting it as your truth allows you to enjoy the other people in your life—the ones who are right there in front of you; the ones who chose to be there with you.

THE BLENDED MANIFESTO

If the children are loved and nourished—mind, body, and soul—and cared for unequivocally by all parties involved, that is what matters most. Everything else is unnecessary. You might not be able to control court orders or custody arrangements, but you can control how you show up as a person, for the kids, for your partner, and for yourself.

CHAPTER 5

Money, Money, Money

(How hard it is to keep money from leading your relationships)

I took on the role of chief financial officer (CFO) for our family early on. Some families split the role, some divide it up, but in our blend, I was handed the responsibility of money manager. I have always paid all our bills. I created the logins, the passwords, the security questions, and I handle the electronic payments. For years I even stamped and addressed a water bill because the company did not accept credit cards or online payments. Another bill I handle on a monthly basis is child support. I have been making my husband's child-support payments for ten years. Just to clarify, I make the payment with *his* money; my man works his ass off and pays for his shit, I'm just the one physically responsible for getting it paid every month.

Child support is an essential payment, and one deserves financial support for taking on the most important job they will ever do—raising the children they had with someone. It's for your child, not you, and that's what everyone seems to forget. Kids don't pay their own way in life. More than just providing the money though, it's putting in the effort. I often wonder why parents who choose not to be present in the upbringing of their child can't at least be financially responsible. You need to hold your ex accountable, but only to the extent that you have the energy to do so. It can be emotionally humiliating and draining to chase them around, asking for money when they aren't being agreeable, or worse, can't be located. And the system is just fucked. It isn't the fault of the person on the other end of the line of Child Support Services. No, they are always sensitive and supportive, and they wish they had better answers for you. It must break their hearts to tell women, "I'm sorry, ma'am, unless you know where he is and how to contact him and whether he wants to be contacted, then there's nothing we can do."

So, I suck it up every month and send the money my husband is legally responsible for paying. You may be wondering why I put myself through it. Maybe I should have told him that it was his bill, so he would need to be the one to make sure it was paid in a timely fashion. Maybe I should have just said no to paying that particular bill. But the way I saw it, if we had made him the CFO, I would have expected him to manage all the bills. In our home, we structured our life around one person being responsible for the finances, and I wasn't going to accept that role and then exclude one bill because I had resentment from my own experience. That seemed childish. And perhaps it was a very early, albeit subconscious way of accepting all the chaos and emotional baggage that comes from marrying a man with an ex-wife and two children. Perhaps it was a version of cutting—it provided me with just enough pain to remind me I was alive. During the first few years, I paid that bill through tears, other times through seething anger, and often with the dread only a second wife can understand. And some months we simply could not afford it. At one point the child-support bill was bigger than our mortgage payment.

You might be wondering, *Why didn't she put that shit on autopay?* There are several reasons, actually. First, the current child-support centers seem to be designed to unfairly penalize fathers who are paying the support but make a mistake along the way, while aiding and abetting the no-job-having-child-support-dodging assholes of the world. Here's how shitty the court systems work for fathers who are actually showing up for their children: At one particularly broke period in our history, just after my husband started his own construction company and then was immediately slapped with a business lawsuit aimed at destroying our family financially, I bounced a child-support check. To this day, my husband can NEVER write a check for child support again. That was six years ago. One check. One time. I miscalculated. I forgot. I thought I had enough days between bill payments. All of the above. We were living off my teacher's salary, which we planned around and saved until we got sued and watched our entire savings go to an attorney overnight. It was a tough time, I accidentally bounced the child-support check, and now I cannot mail a check to the Attorney General to pay my husband's bill. Now, this may not seem like that big of a deal until you realize what a crap system they have for online credit card payments, and that making online payments always triggers a flag on my debit card for fraud, which would shut down my card every month unless I call and confirm the charge to my account. No good deed goes unpunished, my friend.

I did not get it for many years, but I think accepting responsibility for making these payments all those years ago was a way for me to work through my husband's life before me. It forced me to face his past every month. I could be angry about it, or make peace with it, but every month I had a new opportunity to face my own demons and my own insecurities about his life that came before me. I also sat in awe of his financial responsibility to his children. He had committed to a sizable monthly payment and to reimburse all medical costs. Any prescription, any co-pay, any emergency room visit, he is required to shell out 100 percent of the payments. I had a hard time understanding how he had 50 percent custody, yet his court-ordered child support didn't seem to reflect that he would still be financially responsible for his children. My husband has also paid for extracurricular activities, sports registrations, equipment, and uniforms, plus yearbooks, school clothes, supplies, pictures, etc. My husband has always figured out a way to fork over the money for anything his children need and want.

I didn't understand in the beginning how this arrangement was fair. It wasn't. But that's how it goes for fathers who want to keep their children.

The assumption often made in the family court system is that fathers want 50 percent custody so they do not have to pay child support. He was not going to let that be a question for his children. My husband would have his kids 50 percent of the time **and** agree to full child support, in part to prove to the Texas judge he was not just another Walkaway Joe. I couldn't very well be resentful about that, and it was all decided on before I entered the picture anyway. I could fight it, bitch about it, resent his ex-wife for it, cause one million more petty arguments between the two homes, or I could find a way to accept it. Well, you know what I did—Option A for years, bitches!

Eventually, though, I did make peace with it. I received very little in financial support for my son, but my husband was not that man. I came out ahead in the big picture of life. I came to understand that he wasn't paying his ex-wife, he was helping support his children. He was ensuring that in the 50 percent of their life he did not have them, they would still have what they needed. His monthly child-support bill meant he didn't have to worry quite as much when they were gone.

I now even appreciate that child support helps bridge the quality of life between the two homes. My husband's child-support payments mean his ex-wife can live comfortably in a good and safe environment for his children. It helps make sure his children get special events, vacations, and weekend adventures at their mother's home too. It's also much easier to see it that way now because we are more financially stable than we were in the beginning of our marriage. I've been broke, but I'm not right now. Money definitely buys peace of mind because being able to pay your bills on time makes acceptance much easier. Perhaps even in both homes.

If that's not you yet, if you and your partner are still building financial stability and struggling, hang in there. Those were the months of tears and anger. Some months were tighter than others. Sometimes we had to say no. Sometimes we had to borrow money from a parent. People don't walk away from a divorce with more money than they had before it. As we are all creating our blended families, most of us are saddled with debt and bills from our former life. Accept them. Accept the debt; accept the bills. Put a plan together to pay things off or make more money. Try and try again to not let money influence and lead how you interact with each other. And try very hard not to blame each other. Compassion and empathy are everything, even with finances.

When I'm stressing over money, my husband likes to tell me, "Honey, it's just money. We can always make more." This response used to infuriate me. My head would race with thoughts of *What is he talking about? You can't just get more money. Money doesn't work like that. He thinks making money is just so easy.* I get now that he isn't telling me money is not important, he just means arguing over money is not important. He has taught me that money should not lead relationships. If we can pay for something, then we pay for it. If splitting the cost of school pictures saves a kid from having to go back and forth between parents to ask, or if loading up the lunch money account saves everyone from a battle, then so be it.

Next time your stepchild brings home that sign-up sheet, pull out your wallet, or your spouse's wallet, and pay for it. No questions asked. Make sure they have the yearbook, or the Spirit Day T-shirt, or the $2 for Donut Fridays at school, or whatever it is that makes them feel included and excited. Do not ever tell that stepchild that since you pay child support, they can go tell their other parent to pay for it. Do not say that, whether it's over a $14 magazine subscription or a $300 pitching glove. That's not to say you can't say no if you simply don't have it in your budget, but don't say no out of spite and malice. Don't say no in a way that makes that child feel like they are a burden. And don't hate an ex-spouse—you got a man who pays for his shit and is accountable for his responsibilities. At the end of the day, it's just money, and you can always make more.

THE BLENDED MANIFESTO

Don't let money be the bargaining chip that determines how you show up for your family and babies (biological or stepchildren). It is never money that holds relationships together, it is our attitude toward money and the meaning we assign to it.

CHAPTER 6

An Absent Parent

(How hard it is to heal a child after abandonment)

My son was born in 1998 when I was seventeen years old. By the time my high school graduation ceremony rolled around, I was a teen mom with a three-week-old. I went on to graduate from college four years later, on my son's fourth birthday. I finished graduate school four years after that, as he was turning eight. Those eight years are a blur. I was not the mother he deserved. I stayed in an unhealthy relationship for far too long, and for years I let it distract me from raising him. I still struggle with the guilt of allowing that relationship to interfere with my parenting. I was utterly stressed out, every minute of every day. I was pretty much alone in the world except for the saving graces that are my best friends. I lived in survival mode.

When I was four months pregnant with my son, I had a head-on collision with a gravel truck on a dark country road. I was thrown out the back windshield of the car, and I gained consciousness alongside the road, covered in gravel. I had no recollection of the wreck or its aftermath, and the only thing I could remember were the few seconds before impact. In one of those life-altering, slow-motion moments, I remember begging God for us to live. In my bargain with the Universe, I promised that if we could just both live through it, I would give this child everything he deserved. The ambulance showed up and took me to the hospital, where I repeated over and over to every medical person I saw, "I'm pregnant, I'm pregnant, please tell them I'm pregnant." The nurses quickly hooked me up to machines and began looking for a heartbeat. In what felt like an eternity, a heartbeat slowly appeared across the monitor. Never have I sobbed so hard. We were both alive. It was then and there that I committed to becoming the best person and mother I could be. The Universe had told me I was supposed to raise this baby, and I had promised both God and my baby that I would give him the life he deserved, regardless of circumstance.

My son has never really known his biological father. They only met a handful of times before he disappeared altogether. He was supposed to pick him up and take him out for his fourth birthday. No show, no call. Never heard from him again. It was like something out of a bad melodrama, only it was real, and it was happening to my four-year-old. My son sat in the front of our rental house for hours, looking out the window, willing a Walkaway Joe to come back for him. He never did.

My son's biological father and I are from the same small town. We grew up playing at a neighbor's house together when we were just kids. He wasn't a stranger, but he wasn't ever going to be a father either. For years people couldn't wait to give me updates on him whenever I went home. "Have you heard from Walkaway Joe?" or "Did you know Walkaway Joe was just in town last weekend?" It was like a cut that never healed. Every time I went back home, I had to hear about how he was doing, all the while trying to answer questions from a small child about why his father wasn't in the picture. Watching a parent walk away from your child is horrendous. It changes them in ways you can never compensate for, it creates a wound you can't heal for them, and it breaks your heart.

When a parent purposely abandons a child, never to be seen or heard from again, no amount of love and support can fill the void left behind. They are forever changed at their core. They struggle with their own identity, they struggle to love themselves, and they struggle to love other people. There is no quick and easy cure for abandonment. My son and I did not have just one conversation about it, we had hundreds of conversations about it. We talked every time he joined a little league team and boys were warming up with their dads, every time Father's Day rolled around and he had to tell his teacher he didn't have a father to make a gift for, every time he went to a friend's house who had a dad present in the home, every time I could not be everything he needed. All I could do was continuously remind him that it was not his fault, that he was the greatest thing that ever happened to me, and that he would grow up one day and get to be what he never had.

The story I gave my son was that his father was on drugs, and that the drugs were just more powerful than he was. Let me be clear here. While I honestly don't know if that claim is the truth, I couldn't think of any other reason for him to have walked away from this beautiful and amazing little boy, and I had to tell him something. I had to have an answer so that he did not think his father walking away was because of him. I figured it didn't really matter if I tarnished the image of a man who left him waiting on a curb. So, when my son was in the throes of hurt and loss, we prayed for his father. We prayed for him to get help and to get healthy. It gave my son a reason, and he desperately needed that reason so he didn't blame himself.

I struggled with how to raise a boy. My son struggled to believe that someone abandoning him was not his fault. We both struggled to understand how a parent just changes their mind one day. With my own father no longer in my life, and my mother thousands of miles away at the time, we were a family of two. I had an aunt and uncle who stepped up for us when we needed it most, picking up my son for weekends to give me a break and allowing me to pull my shit back together. I am eternally grateful to them. With the exception of one unhealthy long-term relationship when my son was young, it was mostly just the two of us. I never bought into the single-mother myth that your child is your best friend or the idea that it was "us against the world." Those ideas did not work for me because I never wanted him to know his mother was a broke-ass, single teen mom just trying to keep us alive most days.

Our life functioned through structure, systems, and control. Before I became a teacher, I was trapped in a soul-sucking bank job that I hated. However, between the 401K and the bonuses, I was able to purchase a home. Our morning routine was early and rigid. The school bus showed up down the hill at 6:30 a.m., and my son was ready and on it. I then started the hour-long commute into the city where I worked all day. The school bus dropped my son off at the bottom of the hill every day like clockwork, and he walked the one-mile, uphill trek to home. At first, he hated it. He was a little scared and overwhelmed because it was a large hill that the school bus could not attempt. But before long he was calling me every day when he got home to tell me about all the adventures he'd had walking up that hill. I think the trek became therapeutic for him. He'd wander through the woods on his way home each day, just decompressing. To this day, that kid loves to hike through the woods.

When I met my now-husband, I was a new homeowner, a high school English teacher, and a still-single mother of a twelve-year-old. I was doing okay. Life was easing up. We lived in a hill-country cabin on a hill that had a view, a porch swing, and two dogs. It was our little piece of heaven. I had curated a life for my son and myself that I could be proud of. We were living on a teacher's salary, and I was saddled with student loan debt (still am actually), a mortgage payment, and a car payment with the interest rate of a credit card. Money was tight, but we were mostly happy. Dare I even say . . . content?

The day I told my son we were moving in with my boyfriend and his children, he was both excited and scared. He wasn't happy about changing schools, leaving his friends, and moving from our home on the hill. Still, even at thirteen years old, he appreciated what we were trying to create. As selfless as a thirteen-year-old could ever be, my son jumped on board quickly and with relative ease. He let me find love, he accepted becoming a big brother, and he embraced having a father in his life. Looking back, we did not give him enough credit for how gracefully he handled the plateful of change we gave him. Let me correct that error now. My teenage son jumped into his new role in our family with open arms. He was no longer an only child—he had small children looking up to him now. He played with his new siblings until they all laughed themselves into asthma attacks. He was, and still is, an amazing young man. My son was instrumental in creating bonds with his new stepsiblings. His acceptance of my decisions helped glue us together when times got tough, and times most certainly got tough.

...

My son hung up on me the other day, or I hung up on him. I'm not entirely sure who hung up first. We are a lot alike, that kid and me. Big dreams, big personalities, and big insecurities. He's had a rough go of it the last few years. His blended family both helped and hurt his ability to grow and mature. He has his family unit, and he knows where home is, and some time ago he came back home to live with us for a six-month period to sort some things out.

His blended family is his home base, his touchstone in life. The summer after he graduated high school, he moved several hours away. It was incredibly hard on us both. I think he felt like there wasn't a place for him in the home as a newly forming adult. I was certainly up to my eyeballs in the stress of raising three small children at the time, and I wasn't as present for him as I needed to be. Growing up in a blended family, my son gained a father and siblings, and the life of a child in a large, mostly happy family. But he also lost a lot of my attention. There were two little ones, a baby, and a new husband. I just didn't know *how* to give him everything he still needed while working out all the changes I was going through as well. And that's kind of been the story of his life—me trying to be the best mother I can for him while also growing up myself. I haven't always done it very well, and I wish I could go back and do it all over again, correcting the parts I didn't get right the first time around. I know I can't. In the words of John Maxwell, "Life is not a puzzle. You don't get to see the picture before you start."[2] Ain't that the truth, Mr. Maxwell? And maybe it's all for the best. Maybe it's okay that I haven't been everything I wanted for him, but hopefully I've been enough.

He is back on his own again, living alone in an apartment just a few minutes down the road. He has roots, and he knows where he comes from, but in the early years of our blend, during the crucial formative years, our blend did not have our shit together. I'm not sure we even do now, but the pressure was intense those first few years. He was maneuvering all the dynamics of a newly blended family, while also growing into a young man, a young man who had only met his own father a handful of times and hadn't seen him since he was four years old.

Today, he will tell you that my husband is his father, his "dad." Today, he will tell you that being abandoned at such a young age has no effect on who he is now. I will tell you it made a fundamental impact on his soul. I raised him, I watched him hurt, I fought the demons for him as best I could. No matter a mother's efforts to heal a child's broken heart, no amount of triage can bandage the wound that has been caused from a parent who has walked away and chosen to never know their child. Watching my son grow up in a fatherless world was heart-wrenching. It's simply a void that a mother cannot fill. When he learned how to pee, I was the one telling him how to aim. When he wanted to throw a baseball, I was the one who had to learn how to throw a ball. When he kissed a girl for the first time, I was the one who picked him up from the dance. Beyond the stress of trying to be mother and father, there are no words to help a child when a parent chooses to be absent. That is the child's journey, and theirs alone. I could be, and was, involved in every aspect of his life, but when he looked up into the stands, he only ever saw me. Until I met my husband.

I will forever remember the first time they met each other. It was at a little pizza joint after a middle school basketball game. My son sized him up and seemed to approve. They talked about basketball shoes, and I think they were both in love right then and there. I also remember the first time they played catch together. Those two spent hours just throwing a ball back and forth. It's a huge reason why I fell so hard in love with my husband. That, and when he rebuilt my front porch the first Mother's Day after we met. My husband is the absolute best father I have ever met, and for the first time in his life, my son had a man willing to take on the damage of another man's making.

When my son turned thirteen, and for nearly every birthday through his eighteenth, my husband took him and a few of his friends on an annual primitive camping trip. Hell or high water, they would come back from a weekend of man-time, and it would erase whatever hardships their relationship was facing at the time. While my husband has always been present for my son, we didn't just ride off into the sunset. They went through rough patches. A lot of them. We had one grown man trying to find his place in a new and growing family, and one young man trying to find his place in a new and growing family. Power struggles, jealousy, and resentments were not uncommon. But when those two returned from an annual camping trip together, they came back bonded. My husband got to see my son for who he really was, and my son got to have the undivided attention of the man he admired most in his life.

Their journey from strangers to father and son has been a decade in the making. They have both put in the work to get here. It wasn't easy for them—both nursing similar wounds—to lay down the swords and battle armor and love each other. Sometimes it took so much of my energy I thought I would strangle them both. But we saw it through. They saw it through. I am so grateful they did.

THE BLENDED MANIFESTO

While you cannot and will not replace the presence or the void left by an absent parent in the lives and hearts of your own child(ren) or stepchild(ren), you can create a new bond. One that is stronger than any biological equation. A bond built on effort, trust, love, and choice. A chosen parent and a chosen child.

CHAPTER 7

Birth Order

(How hard it is to be the parent with the oldest child)

When our kids are young, we harbor fantasies of the perfect children we will raise. While silently judging every parent we come across, we assure ourselves that our child will never act like *that*. When our children are young, we naïvely believe our precious babies will forever stay the chubby, cherub-faced heart-snatchers we have come to adore. But by the time we have raised teenagers, the jig is up. The fantasy is over. Reality appears, and we are forced to accept the cold and hard truth that our children are their own individual human beings. Ultimately, we are just here to guide them and keep them as safe as possible. We must step away from the presumption that we know what our children will and will not do with their lives. We do not know who they will become, what they will choose to do, or how they will get there. As parents of older children, we must learn to eat a lot of crow and to make peace with the unknown, which is precisely why being the parent of the oldest child is particularly challenging in a blended family.

While I was raising a teenager, my husband had only been a parent for a few years. Having only parented toddlers, he still believed his son would never quit giving him kisses and hugs in the drop-off line at preschool. He still believed his children would always love him, that they would never tell him how much they hated him, and that they would forever be able to talk about anything together. Like most parents of young children, he still had hope.

Having the oldest child in the blend is tough. You learn firsthand all the shittiest parts of parenting because you are the first to parent through all the hardest bits. You also get to do it under the critical gaze of your spouse who still believes *his* young children will *never* act like *that*. If you are the one with the oldest child, it brings about additional resentments to overcome later on in the marriage. Your child will be the first to learn to drive, get a speeding ticket, date, have sex, break curfew, sneak out, get caught drinking at a party, get in trouble at school, talk back to a teacher, go to prom, graduate, move out, move back in, and on and on and on. As a stepparent, it is quite easy to sit on the sidelines with the belief that you know how to parent these situations while honestly believing that your child will never act in such a way.

Before you go nominating yourself for a best-parent-ever award, may I suggest you slow your roll a minute. You will be proven wrong. I'm not suggesting there aren't great teenagers in the world. I'm also not suggesting that if your teenager finds themselves in one, or all, of the aforementioned scenarios that they are not wonderful human beings with a great future ahead of them. I am stating, however, that our children will mess up. There will be big mistakes, and little ones, but they are just children trying to learn how to grow up. Mistakes are made because it is how they learn. They are human, and they are navigating their way in this world just like we once did. So, a little grace, humor, and compassion will win you some brownie points in their books as they continue to experience the roller coaster that is life. It is very easy in a blended family to start pitting teenager against teenager in an effort to prove ourselves as parents. Pitting any family member against one another never helps a blend create a bond. *All* your kids have different stories, different hurts, different expectations, and different timelines. Do not judge, and do not compare, at least not if you want your family to create a bond over the next couple decades.

Even the most reflective partner can be guilty of judging how a spouse parents an older child. It is biological nature to believe your children are better than someone else's. In a blended family, your spouse is the "someone else." It's nearly impossible for a stepparent who hasn't raised teenagers to carry your load with you, or offer insight into the best parenting decision, or understand the parenting difficulties you are facing. If you are the stepparent of a teenager, try not to be displeased with your spouse in these moments; instead, try to hear them out and take in their opinions and ideas. Experience is the best teacher, and parents of young children simply do not have the experience to know how hard raising teenagers can be until they cross that bridge with their own biological children. We want to look to our spouse as our partner in life, but in a blended family, that doesn't necessarily include parenting. Eventually, you will have to make your own parenting decisions based on the love you have for your child and what feels right as their parent. Consequently, when those younger stepchildren finally show themselves for the teenage demons they all are, you will have to step aside and allow your spouse to parent as they see fit. You cannot be the one swooping in to save the day. Allow them to grow together during this phase.

Given that there is a biological belief in the greatness of your own child, an added weight of raising the oldest child in the blend occurs when your stepchildren do eventually grow up to do all the stupid shit that teenagers do, and that subsequently also becomes your own child's fault. It is almost guaranteed that your child will at some point become the scapegoat for your stepchildren's behavior, and your spouse will cite the belief that your child set a bad example for the younger ones. Whether it's as small as holding a fork incorrectly or talking back, or something as life altering as an unplanned pregnancy, if you have the oldest child, it is highly likely your child will be blamed if the younger kids find themselves in the same scenarios. Try not to totally hate your spouse when this happens. Try to offer understanding about how hard parenting teenagers can be, and ultimately choose to forgive and forget.

What no parent really wants to face when raising teenagers is that their days of parenting as they know them are coming to an end with their children. When your child becomes a teenager, your parenting role in their life is completely uprooted. They don't need you in the same ways. Quite honestly, they don't want you around in the same ways. The change is as jarring for the child as it is for the parents involved. In a blended family, the stepparent is typically less emotionally affected by this fact. A stepparent can take the emotion out of raising teenagers in a way a biological parent may not be able to. If you are going through these parental changes first in your family, check your expectations of your spouse. They do not have the same biological heartstrings for your teenager that you do. They will not lead with their heart the way you will when you look at your baby-boy-turned-young-man, which certainly doesn't mean they do not love your child, but it may very well mean they cannot support you through the process.

Teenagers are dumb asses, plain and simple. They love you but simultaneously hate themselves for it, as if it is a betrayal to their future adult self for finding any value whatsoever in you and your parenting. It's a shit show inside their heads and their hearts. They are afraid and anxious, yet they are pretending to be brave and grown. They are ready to take on the world but are secretly hoping they can run away from it. It's a rite of passage, a coming-of-age act to assert your independence as you navigate your teenage years. Allow your teens to experience this rite of passage and, in the meantime, try not to get your heartstrings in a tizzy. I promise they will still need you when shit hits the fan. The mind of a teenager is confused and lost before you ever add the stresses of a blended family. They were genetically wound up before you handed them the dynamics of a new family to manage. Teens have it tough, and we usually forget just how tough. We forget how absolutely insane and out of control our lives felt in high school. For many of us, we forget because it was so traumatizing that we had to block it out. Teenagers are managing life introductions to social graces, bullying, social media, sexuality, pregnancies, abuse, pornography, alcohol, drugs, driving, and education, to name but a few. All the while, they are ultimately at the mercy of the adults in their lives to help them through it.

Teenagers already have trust issues with the world because the world as they know it completely flips on them. Add in the trust issues caused by a blended family, and we wonder why a teenager may not be the easiest person to be around. Teens have to face their own emerging sexuality (not to mention the cocktail of hormones that is having a block party in their bodies) as well as the jarring realization that their parents have a sex life. Additionally, teenagers have a difficult time expressing themselves and their true feelings. They can't form and enunciate an entire sentence because their synapses are actually evolving at such a speed that their mind can't keep up. Then, add in the expectation of being emotionally available to bond with a new family. If you take a moment and sit with these facts, you will see that it is kind of asking a lot from a human being who knows next to nothing about the world around them.

Trust me when I say that teenagers are literally doing their best to remember how to put one foot in front of the other some days. I did not always recognize the challenges my own teens were facing in life, let alone in their blended families. I only recognize it now because I have done it three times, in three highly varying circumstances. Teenagers are fucking crazy. They are irrational, unintentional, somewhat ungrateful, moderately loving, and significantly confused. Teenagers are the perpetual manifestation of the first moment when you turn on a light in a dark room. You know it is going to happen, but you are still stunned and confused by the brightness. Our teens are frequently stunned and confused. Everything is new, and it's equal parts exciting and terrifying. Even when they know they are growing up, they are still stunned and confused by it all. Imagine feeling that way on a daily basis. I know you can. You were a teen once.

Having the oldest child in the blend opens you up to a host of marital resentments down the road. While I did the parenting of my son when he was a teenager, I often enforced what my husband *and* I decided our expectations in the home were. Or, at least, that's what I thought I was doing. When his turn rolled around many years later, I naturally assumed we would have the same expectations and that he would now enforce them. He did not. His expectations had changed.

My son was expected to do a lot around the house. Still, my husband thought he needed more chores. I allowed his expectations to lead my parenting because I believed we were enforcing the expectations of our home, not just the expectations for my son. I was wrong. When my stepchildren became teenagers, my husband adopted a very different take on parenting than he had eight years prior. Resentments damn near took me over.

If I so much as picked up a dish after dinner when my son was a teen, my husband reminded me to let my son do it. I took that to mean that as a family, we believed our children should regularly contribute to the home and doing the dishes would be their contribution to dinner. Fast-forward eight years. I found myself sucker-punched when my teenage stepchildren were rarely expected to handle dinner dishes, or chores in general. My son scoured bathrooms every weekend, was expected to clean up after dinner, fed and watered the dogs daily, swept the home weekly, took out the trash regularly, and did his own laundry. If his grades dropped below a B, he had additional chores and lost all privileges until they improved. He was also required to have a part-time job if he wanted the privilege of driving. As my stepchildren have become teenagers, my husband's perspective on chores and grades has drastically changed. I have struggled to forgive him, and myself.

I do not carry guilt for expecting my son to contribute to the running of our house. I firmly believe children need to be held accountable to responsibilities in the home. However, I greatly struggled with guilt over allowing someone else's influence to dictate my parenting decisions. My son would have had chores regardless, but he likely would not have had so many.

I likely would have shown him more grace when he forgot about them or left the house without completing them all. I came on hard and strong because I was under the assumption that it was how *we* were raising *our* children. When that script was flipped, I was left asking myself why the expectation was okay for my son but not for my husband's kids.

Today, my son will tell you he is grateful for the responsibility expected of him when he was younger. His roommate will tell you he appreciates having a roommate who knows how to clean a house, and I hope his future wife will someday appreciate that he does laundry, knows his way around a home, and makes an equal partner, but none of that soothes a mother's guilty conscious for allowing a new husband to set the expectations for how I parented. I have struggled a lot with forgiving my husband for the double standard shown to my son.

Our family was so new back then. I felt like I was sacrificing nearly everything I had to make this new family work. It hurts my heart to admit that one of those sacrifices was how I parented my child. I accepted someone else's expectations of how my child should be raised—someone who had only been in this parenting gig a few years at the time, someone who still believed his children would never act like *that*—instead of trusting my own intuition and letting my child's energy lead the way. There I was handling a teenager while taking the advice of someone parenting toddlers.

I also didn't yet have the insight to recognize just how much my new husband was struggling in his new stepdad role. I did not yet know the internal battle he was managing inside his own mind. I did not yet know the extent to which his own demons were fighting themselves. It was only later that he was able to open up about the triggers becoming a stepdad brought up for him. I did not yet know how hard it was for him to sort through years of living with an abusive stepdad, while at the same time also learning how to be a stepdad himself. If I had known, if I could have had insight into what he was experiencing emotionally on a daily basis, I could have handled the situation more effectively. I could have taken his input, politely filed it away for future reference, then followed my own parenting arrow. My own immaturity never allowed me to consider that my husband may be struggling through the changes in our life as well. I just thought the extra chores, the additional expectations, and the new responsibilities were the compromises that all newly blended families had to make, and when those compromises were not reciprocated years later, I found myself unshakably angry.

What I've come to appreciate is that the differences in parenting, then versus now, also have much to do with time and circumstance. Had my husband parented his teenage children that many years ago, his parenting may have looked similar to how he parented my son. Throughout our marriage, we have healed so many parts of ourselves thanks to our family and our relationship. Everything was harder those first few years of marriage because we didn't know each other, nor did we fully know or understand ourselves. The demons my husband and I have been able to heal from because of our life together have drastically affected how we show up in the world for each other and for our children.

I have found forgiveness, and I have mostly let go of the resentments. My son and my husband have a beautiful relationship today. They are father and son, they have a friendship, and they are bonded within each other's lives. None of that happened accidentally. As the adults leading our family, we have had to really face our anger, our resentments, and our past traumas. We had to want to figure them out; we had to want to let go of the dark clouds lingering around our home and inside our guts. I still find myself resentful when doing dishes after dinner, and my head is filled with anger. Sometimes I let it control me, and I cannot shut it down. Sometimes I can distract my mind just long enough to count to one hundred or go into another room for thirty minutes until I can have rational thoughts again. When I can pull my brain out of the spiral, I remember I have already learned this lesson. I have already forgiven myself and my husband. When I can remember that

I do not have to continue reliving this particular battle, I let go and love my family in that moment. Then, and only then, can I tell the nearest teenager around to get over here and do these dishes.

THE BLENDED MANIFESTO

Forgive yourself for the decisions you made with what you knew at the time. You were doing your best. You are doing your best. And when in doubt, take a few moments away, breathe, recollect who you are, and trust your parental instincts.

CHAPTER 8

The Pink Cupcake

*(How hard it is to keep your "our baby"
from being lost in the shuffle)*

My husband and I knew early on in our relationship that we wanted to have an "our baby." We moved in together in June, and I went off birth control in August. We said we would give it sixty days to see what happened. Apparently, I am quite fertile. Two weeks later I was pregnant. Long before I met my husband, I had told the world I wanted four kids and a house full of crazy. Well, that's exactly what I got.

Given how accepting my son had been through all the other recent upheaval, I fully expected him to embrace having a sibling of his own. He did not. His exact words? "You two are total idiots. We don't need another kid in this house. I will never love this baby." Being the fearless and mature leaders we were, we went into the bathroom and cried, terrified that the thirteen-year-old had more sense than we did. After we peeled ourselves off the floor, we recited all the reasons why we had made the decision to bring a baby into our world, and we officially grew our family to the size of a basketball team, alternate included.

We wanted something that everyone felt a part of, something that bonded us all together and rounded us out as a family. The baby would be a beautiful gift to our children and ourselves, something that everyone in our new family felt they belonged to in a permanent way. We believed having a baby together would solidify our status as a family. That our "our baby" would be the bridge that connected both our families together. Our little pink cupcake did indeed show us that no matter how tough creating a family gets, we all belonged to each other.

A few months into my pregnancy, back before gender-reveal parties were setting states on fire and killing grandmothers, we brought home a pink cupcake for my then-teenage son. It was our peace offering to tell him he would have a little sister. This time he cried, then yelled at us for not giving him a brother because how was he going to teach a girl how to play basketball? He then dropped the cupcake in the trash. We again retreated to the bathroom to cry.

Things did not go much better when we were ready to tell my stepchildren because that meant we first had to tell the ex-wife. She also cried, then yelled so loudly over the phone that my then-boyfriend had to walk into the garage to finish the conversation so his crazy, pregnant girlfriend did not hear the things being said on the other end of the line.

Finally, we only had the two littles left to tell. By now, we were at least conditioned for how badly the conversation might go. Armed with the strength of love, we went in for one final battle. The littles could not have been happier. Screams of pure joy sent some much-needed shockwaves through our hearts. Maybe we weren't total idiots after all. Maybe, just maybe, this "our baby" would be the heart that connected all our hearts together.

As the house started filling up with the one million things it takes to bring something home that will literally not roll over for six months, our relationship started showing signs of cracking. He—a newly divorced father of two—was now stepping into a family of six. Me—an independent perfectionist—was now wholly dependent on another person. He started coming home late, staying out and drinking, and I started feeling relief on nights he did not come home until after all the kids were in bed. The gravity of how we had uprooted our lives over one year, and without all that much prior reflection or consideration, began to weigh heavily on both of us.

By then, my son had started coming around to the idea of having a new baby in the family and even went to some doctor appointments with us. It was at one such appointment when my son picked up a contraption sitting on the counter in the exam room. Mistaking it for a seashell, he proceeded to put it up to his ear to try to hear the ocean. "I can't hear anything," he said. "That's because it's a vagina," my husband said back. The horror on my son's adolescent face broke through all the tensions we had been battling in life. We burst out into uncontrollable laughter and were obnoxiously guffawing when the doctor entered the room. It was in that moment, through the bellyaching, snot-inducing laughter, that we finally got to address what my thirteen-year-old had been so terribly angry about. Just as he was hitting his prepubescent stride, he was struck with the knowledge that his mother was having a sexual relationship, and it had produced a baby. The move, the new siblings, the new school, and the new home all proved infinitely easier to accept in his thirteen-year-old brain than facing the fact that his mother was having sex.

Once it was all out in the open, we were able to start moving forward. He wanted to feel my belly when the baby was moving, he helped us put the crib together, and he even decided that maybe he could teach a girl to play basketball after all. Everything was finally coming together. Clearly, we had this; we knew what we were doing. How could we have ever doubted ourselves? Our blend would be better than any blend that ever existed because our love was stronger and better than any that came before.

We brought our little pink cupcake into the world on June 6, 2012. My son was at the hospital with us, while my stepchildren anxiously awaited the arrival of their new baby sister at home. My most cherished family photo is of all six of us about two minutes after we walked through the door on the day we brought her home from the hospital. We all gathered around her in awe, and we all simultaneously fell in love with her. She is the manifestation of all the reasons we wanted to add an "our baby" to our family. She is my son's baby sister, and he loves her completely. She is her sister's best friend and closest confidant. She holds her other brother's heart in her hand, and she is our daughter.

I am not exactly sure how souls get sent to us, but I am convinced that she handpicked us. I imagine her watching the train wreck we created down here and telling God that she was up for the challenge. She is the heart and glue of our family. She shows forgiveness and compassion when I do not think I have any left. She is our rock, and I only hope she doesn't grow up feeling the pressure of being a caretaker to all. She already carries the weight of our world for us on some days.

She has had to learn what transition days mean, and how to FaceTime her sister when she is not home. She is fascinated with the fact that her dad was married to her siblings' mother, sometimes asking so many questions that I literally run out of appropriate answers. She tries to understand why there are different rules for her than her siblings, and she continues to do it with a grace I can only aspire to. As she gets older, she is handling a whole different set of dynamics for understanding her family. She is still a blended child. Since she can remember, she has been forced to face the harsh reality that not all families stay together, and she sometimes struggles with anxiety over it all. Her family has specific needs, and she is growing beautifully as we try to keep up with her.

I would be remiss if I did not admit that there are times when raising a blended family gets so hard that I don't know if I can keep doing it. Right or wrong, sharing a baby together has pushed me to work through the hardest seasons in our life. I do not know if I would have been able to push through had we not had a child together. It's easy to believe your stepchildren would be better off if you were not married to their father. I am not saying it's true, but it's easy to let yourself believe that, especially on the hard days. It is not so easy to believe when it's a biological child. When my marriage goes through dark moments, I have a recurring thought about what would happen to her, to her siblings' relationship with her, to her relationship with her father, and to her relationship with me. These thoughts make up the few seconds I need to reevaluate my haste and figure out a way to work through the difficult days. When working through them is not a viable option, the thoughts shift to ones of acceptance and surrender to it all—to our beautiful, chaotic, messy, yet unique blend. Blended families require an infinite amount of acceptance, and our pink cupcake inspires me every single day.

THE BLENDED MANIFESTO

Your family—the one you are choosing to create day after day—is whole. Surrender to the love that exists within each of you. You are each the glue that holds this family together, by choice and by action.

CHAPTER 9

Birthdays, Bedtimes, and Bullshit

*(How hard it is to navigate through every
person needing something different)*

I considered calling this chapter "In the Shit" because at some point many years into your journey, you wake up and ask yourself, "WTF just happened?" In the blink of an eye, I went from being a single mom of one, to dating a guy, to having four kids, to *Good Lord, Sweet Mother of God, how am I going to get through all this a sane person?* It's so hard to see clearly when you are in the shit of it all. That day in, day out of backpacks, homework, progress reports, teacher conferences, calls from the principal, school fundraisers, school shots, medications, after-school practices, physicals, forgotten homework, cavities, braces, playdates, groceries, laundry, chores, and washing assholes kind of shit. No matter your parental role in it all, at some point it's close to sending us all over the edge. It is not easy to get caught up in the shit of it all without losing optimism.

The daily trudge of trying to keep everything together is a tightrope walk. Not only are we not supposed to lose our shit but we are also supposed to continue growing as parents, as couples, as humans. For those hard-core years of parenting when our kids need everything from us, not only are we expected to keep them alive and send the best possible human into the world but we are also supposed to simultaneously become the best humans we can be. Being a parent takes a toll on one's psyche. During those years when our children are young and needy, and as loveable as they will ever be, we are mostly just trying to make it through the day without an internal meltdown.

Case in point, my sock drawer is currently overflowing with teenybopper socks. Intentionally mismatched, lime green and hot pink. No, I do not have a Forever 21 sock fetish. I just have a teenage daughter who *does*, and the genetic belief that you do not waste a good sock. My stepdaughter was born with a concrete phobia of sock seams. The first four and a half years of being her stepmom, I must have survived no less than 3,431 full-on migraine-inducing screaming meltdowns over where the God-forsaken sock seam fell on her toes. Oh. My. God. This girl seriously made the dogs howl as she flailed around, pulling at her sock seam whenever she was expected to put on a shoe. The boys stuffed socks in their ears to dull the sound of their little sister's fury. We bargained, we bribed, and we begged, but she did not budge on her hatred of sock seams. Funny twist . . . a few years into the semi-regular meltdowns, we found out she was doing the exact same thing with her mother. Seriously. Mind blown.

For years I had naturally assumed that the Sock War of 2012 had started as a very deliberate game of Fuck You, Lady, You Are Not My Mother. Of course that's what I believed. It's the only narrative I knew. I did not have conversations with the step-wife back then. My stomach churned when I had to stand in her general vicinity. I am not exaggerating when I say my skin burned and my body temperature rose when we had to talk. I see you ladies nodding—y'all know the feeling I am describing. And I know she felt the same way about me. We were new at it. We were not as evolved, much less healed, and both still stuck in a lot of the hurts and resentments. And that's okay.

At some point, regardless of the mutual hatred then spewing between us, we were forced to combine forces for Operation Seamless Sock. Our mental *in*stability depended on it. I do not remember how it came up, but the step-wife and I were accidentally having a decent conversation at some child's sporting event when the topic moved to none other than our very own sock princess. Step-wife was having the exact same problem as I was. Our mutual sock monster had been exposed for the double agent she was. We were both facing mornings of sock mania, pitchy screams, and lots of tears . . . mostly from us. To this day, if either one of us stumbles upon a rack of seamless socks, we stock up and send pictures with heart emojis to the other.

This revelation would be one of many uncovered between the two houses. Once we finally started talking to each other, we realized a lot of what the adults had projected onto the children as a direct result of the other home just simply wasn't true. Most of the accusations leveraged against the other home were just annoying kid shit—your basic testing of boundaries, trying to get control, or feeling out of control. "Does he say x, y, and z to you too?" and "Does she do x, y, and z to you too?" Time and time again, once we just started talking to each other about the stupid, annoying things our kids were doing, we realized they were doing it at both houses. It had not been an attack against me personally as a human being in their life, or against their father for marrying me, or against their mother for that matter. They were kids being kids who were leveraging both sides of the playing field.

We assumed for years that all subpar behavior was a direct result of the other home's parenting. We were flat-out wrong. The kids' asshole behaviors were just basic asshole behaviors. They were kids learning how to maneuver their own world and trying to learn what the world expects of them. It is just a whole lot harder for kids to learn when they have two different homes to learn it from. The inconsistencies in my stepchildren's lives made for some tough behaviors. But truth be told, the adults were the ones creating the environment; the kids were just trying to figure it all out.

Good ol' human conversation never hurts anybody. The more we adults talked about the behaviors we were struggling with, the more it helped us change some of that behavior. It became harder for the kids to pit each home against each other, and we do not accept those behaviors as easily anymore. We are better at calling out the kids when they try to play both homes. We now say to them, "I know that's not okay at your dad's/mom's house either" or "I know your dad/mom wouldn't be okay with that either" as opposed to the years of saying, "Your mother may put up with that, but I won't in this house" or "Your dad lets you do whatever you want." In fact, recently, in an argument involving both homes, I said to my stepdaughter (in front of her mother), "Your mom and I have worked way too hard to get along to let you come in and try to break that down." Her mother thanked me. We *have* worked that hard, all three of us adults. And all four of our kids have benefited from watching us grow and be better.

By talking openly without any judgment, and learning to communicate better between the homes, we also got to share all the awesome parts of the kids. I remember the hardest part of being a single mother was sitting alone at practices, sporting events, and school plays. I didn't have anyone to share a comment or a moment of pride with about the child on stage. I never got to share the joy of watching my child participate in sports and standing up to cheer with someone who loved him as much as I did. I was alone at most of my son's events, so I could empathize when Step-wife was there alone. She had family and loved ones who would show up as well, but not having that spouse, that other person to see and witness your children from the same perspective of love that you do, is tough. I know what kind of lonely that felt like. Today, we sit together, save each other a seat, and look forward to catching up. We even sometimes get dirty looks from my husband for talking too much and not paying enough attention to the kids' games. But come on, how many hours of baseball can you watch in one day?

I can fully appreciate that some families may never be capable of such a relationship. Those are not the ones I am talking to here. I am talking to *you,* the one reading this book, the one who desires this type of family dynamic within your own blend and wants to make it your own. I am talking to the ones who may be able to get there but need a little motivation to keep trying. Keep changing. Keep forgiving. Keep going. When you are in the shit, when your kids require nearly every ounce of your energy, it is really easy to forget everyone else is there too, sitting in that same pile of shit. That includes a friend, a coworker, a spouse, or an ex. The sad truth of it all is that sometimes we are all too willing to show a stranger more support than our ex, and sometimes we give strangers more grace than our own spouses. Often, it is the people closest to us who get overlooked the most because we are so in the shit that we can't see anyone's struggle but our own. Unfortunately, the only fix may be your kids getting older and freeing up some of your hard-earned headspace. Well, that and mutual love and respect.

Birthday celebrations have evolved as much as any other part of our family. A few years ago, while I was planning my stepdaughter's birthday party, she decided she did not want two of everything anymore. Namely, she was putting a stop to having two birthday parties. How could she be expected to invite friends to two birthday parties or, alternatively, decide at which home she wanted to hold it? I had to agree. Birthdays are tricky in blended families, especially as the kids get older and want their friends involved. So, Step-wife and I joined forces once more to give our girl what she wanted. For the last three years, my stepdaughter has invited a handful of girls to have a birthday party at a local resort near our homes. We rent a room in a hotel with a heated pool because she is a Christmas baby. Yes, *we*. Step-wife and I chaperone the slumber party together. The girls run around, harassing everyone and swimming, playing Truth or Dare with the midnight cleaning crews, and wreaking havoc, all in the name of a slumber party. Step-wife and I find the nearest bar and treat each other like human beings. Like grown women. Like the damn PTA mothers who are learning to accept one another, laying down their armor in the common binding force that is their children.

The first year was tricky. Step-wife and I were new to spending any real time around each other. It was not exactly like hanging out with a friend because (as you can imagine) there were many off-limit topics that neither of us were willing to discuss. I was obviously not going to vent about the last time my husband pissed me off or make inappropriate jokes about my sex life to her (although now I would definitely do both of these things). But we managed. We had fun. We have even been able to open up to each other about things I would never have seen coming. Knowing someone as a whole person makes it a lot harder to hate them. Most importantly, my stepdaughter gets to have birthday parties exactly how she wants them. She does not have to feel torn apart over what should be a celebration of her.

I am certainly not presuming a good relationship can happen in all blended families, or that if it doesn't, they have somehow failed or not tried hard enough. I am just here to say that I know it can happen, and I believe it can happen far more often than it does. I know you can go from hate to love in a decade. I am simply saying that if there is a chance, any whisper of a chance, then do it. Forge a relationship; build a friendship when possible. Whether it's with the ex or the new spouse, it is possible to put down the sword long enough to get to know someone—long enough to see them as human and not hate them because of the technicality that they are "the ex" or the "new spouse." It's super hard and requires a lot of mature adult decisions that we would rather not have to make. But for some of us, with enough effort from both sides, it is a viable option. After all, you may both end up being around for a very long time. If we can take some of the bullshit out of our lives over the years, it is well worth the effort it takes to get there.

Birthdays and plain old kid bullshit do not a ballbuster make, especially in a blended family. Bedtime is a whole new level of the game and is something of "a thing" with me. I take bedtime very seriously. It signals the bell that my workday is over, so nothing comes between me and a bedtime ritual. In twenty-two years of parenting, I have not changed my stance on the benefit of a good bedtime routine. When the kids were younger, I had no problem saying no to any invitation that meant a late bedtime. When my son was young, before the days of cell phones and digital cable boxes, I would set all the clocks in the house ahead by one hour. Then, when he begged to stay up later, I could always say yes, make myself the hero, and still get him to bed on time. (He doesn't find this story nearly as funny as I do.) I am also a creature of habit, so I tried to approach bedtime rituals with all the children just the same way. Instead, it became yet another lesson in why you can't treat them all identically.

My mother read to me every single night without fail, and I continued this tradition with my son. When my daughter reached the age of being able to sit still, I started the same ritual all over again with her. Bedtime stories every single night. I do not have the same ritual with my stepdaughter as I do with my biological daughter. I did when she was younger, but as my biological daughter got older, it became more challenging to handle both bedtimes with such drastically different needs and wants.

As the girls aged, I tried to read to them at the same time, but they just got into fights with each other. When they were together, bedtime reading ultimately turned into a competition for attention between both girls instead of the routine I needed so I could clock out for the day.

I tried reading to each of them separately, but the logistics never worked. By the time I read a chapter to one girl, then went into the other's bedroom to do it again, she would inevitably be half asleep, and quite frankly, I'd be tired of reading and be ready for bed as well. Also, my biological daughter was home every night, and her sister was home half of the nights. It did not seem fair to change my daughter's bedtime routine depending on who was home. It always felt like there was no winning.

I spent bedtimes feeling torn between the two routines and failing at both. At some point I had to make a conscious choice to step away from putting my stepdaughter to bed. I decided I would read to my daughter, tuck in my stepdaughter, and leave my husband to create his own bedtime routine with my stepdaughter. I still cringe with guilt a little bit every time I go to tuck her in, kiss her forehead, tell her good night, and leave. Guilt is as much a part of parenting as it is stepparenting. That part I don't think ever goes away.

These kinds of choices are not easy or taken lightly. Ultimately, I had to put my biological daughter first with the knowledge that I am the only mother she has. I have to trust that my stepdaughter's parents do the same for her. I couldn't deprive my own daughter of something I valued because it meant a different nightly ritual for her than my stepdaughter. As parents in blended families, we face these kinds of choices daily. There is no good or right answer when deciding how to parent versus stepparent. We just have to do what causes our hearts the least amount of strain.

THE BLENDED MANIFESTO

It's okay to do what causes your heart the least amount of strain. It's healthy to let go of the guilt when you feel like you have to choose between kids, every single day. It's okay to choose love, and it's sure as hell okay for that love to look and feel different with each child and person in your blended family.

CHAPTER 10

Hugs, Snuggles, and I Love Yous

(How hard it is to learn how to love someone else's child)

Here's another hard part about being in a blended family: There isn't a right or wrong way to do things or to show one another you care. But there's a difference when those very natural instincts are challenged because of life circumstances. Whenever my biological daughter or son walk into the room, I greet them with open arms. It's not even a conscious thought; I just do it. Instinctively. If my daughter is standing next to me as we wait in line at the grocery store, I pull her close and put my arms around her. When my son stops by unannounced, I grab his neck and tell him I love him. Affection is a natural instinct for most parents. In a blended family, however, that instinct is challenged—challenged by boundaries, biology, and past history and experiences. It is a minefield that one constantly navigates.

Affection is another source of resentment and hurt for children and adults in a blended family. I tuck my daughter into bed every night—with hugs, snuggles, and I love yous. Most nights I do the same with my stepchildren. But the gap between every single night and most nights can feel like a cavern. Sometimes my stepdaughter doesn't want me anywhere near her, and sometimes I don't want to reach out to her either. There are nights when I just don't feel like tucking in my stepchildren, giving them a final good-night, or saying our I love yous. These nights are always a direct result of unresolved conflict from the day. Sometimes it's just because of an ongoing distance our family is currently struggling through. If I'm being honest (and Lord knows I'm trying to be), even bad behaviors and family struggles don't stop me from tucking in my biological daughter every single night. *That* isn't even a conscious thought or choice. Yet family circumstances do sometimes stop me from walking into the other two bedrooms for a final good-night.

Affection in a blended family can cause a hidden explosive to detonate. Whether it's not happening at all, or just not enough for our liking, showing affection can be a significant source of conflict. There were countless times I inwardly raged at my husband when he told all his kids "I love you" before leaving the house, only to skip over my then-teenage son without so much as a good-bye. I know now it had everything to do with fear and nothing to do with love for my son, but that's not what it felt like while it was happening. It felt like our marriage was doomed, like there was no chance this experiment of a family would work if the children involved didn't feel loved. And that part was indeed true. There was no chance of our family bonding if the children didn't feel loved. It's the reasons why my husband was struggling that I got wrong. It was only once my husband could open up about why he was so afraid, why he was having more flashbacks of growing up in his own blended family, and why he didn't know how to show my son he loved him that they could begin their healing.

I have also raged inside my head on the rare occasions that my husband tucks my stepchildren in but forgets to go into our daughter's room. Likewise, I encounter his disappointment on the nights I have skipped over his children when tucking in our daughter. These are the types of nitty-gritty details that make blended families so tumultuous. We deal with more emotional baggage in a thirty-minute bedtime routine than other families take on in an entire year. Even the simplest act of putting children to bed can elicit anger, hurt, frustration, and resentment, all of which bleeds into the precious downtime marriages so desperately need. Instead of snuggling into bed together, blending parents may often silently fume themselves to sleep over who didn't tuck whose kid into bed.

When we meet our partner's child for the first time, we truly don't have the ability to instantly love that child. We may barely know the person we are currently dating, and we sure don't know their child yet. Learning to love a spouse's child is not like loving a biological child, or even a niece or nephew. Our love for a niece or nephew is a given. Assuming there is a healthy history between you and your siblings, you will most likely easily fall in love with their children because you have already loved them. We love our siblings, and therefore, we fall in love with our siblings' children. Even if our nieces and nephews act like brats sometimes, we still want to run around and play with them. We still want to have special handshakes and tell them childhood secrets about their parents. The same is not true with stepchildren. We do not meet our stepchildren with a history of love backing the relationship. We begin the relationship with our stepchildren as strangers, having no prior knowledge of each other or our histories, which is exactly why taking the time to grow the relationship is so critical to our stepchildren feeling love from a stepparent.

The tricky part is that kids grow up so damn fast, and there really isn't all that much time to grow our bond with them. The time equation begins to dwindle when you figure in any shared custody, plus the time they want to bond with their biological parent, leaving us with very little opportunity to give the relationship the time it deserves. Thus, being intentional is crucial to bonding with your blended family, whether it is events put on the family calendar months in advance or weekly little traditions you create. Regardless of what we choose to do, we must be intentional about carving out the time to bond with our stepchildren. Otherwise, it may take significantly longer to create a history with each other that fosters a solid relationship.

The hard truth is that all children deserve to always feel special in their own homes, to know that they are a priority, and that the people chosen to be in their lives love them. What we as stepparents must come to understand, and forgive ourselves for, is that love will look different with our stepchildren. Your heart will melt in a way for your biological children that it may not for your stepchildren. And that's okay. Our biological kids deserve to feel that closeness with their parents. That does not mean you cannot grow your love for your stepchildren. Much the way your love for your spouse grows over the years, your love for your stepchildren can—and I would argue *should* and *will*—also grow over the years.

Do not discount the significance of your relationship with that stepchild. You do matter, and how you treat them will form how they bond with people as adults. If you shun them, you will teach them that they are hard to love. If you work on your connection, you will teach them that they are worthy of love. Hugging your stepchildren may not feel as natural as it does with your own children, but do it anyway. When I walk by my stepdaughter and grab her by the arm and hold her close to me for as long as she will let me, that matters. It matters to her, it matters to me, it matters to my husband. It may not be instinctual, but I do not believe she needs it any less.

My husband struggled with learning how to show my son love and affection. Given his own experience of growing up in a highly disconnected blended family, he had never been shown how to love someone else's child. It took many explosions to explain to my husband that it was hard enough for my son to grow up without a father, but it was damn near destructive to grow up with a father in the home and still feel like he didn't have a dad. In the beginning of my marriage with my husband, my son watched three children have a wonderful dad, while he felt like an outsider. Our first few years together, I had many moments when I questioned my marriage because of the emotional distance between my son and my husband. I felt like I had finally been able to offer my son the family he never had, but then all he could do was window-shop in the father section. It took some counseling for them, many arguments between us, and a lot of time for my husband to get comfortable with loving someone else's child. His struggle was a very real result of his own upbringing by his stepfather—further proof that how you treat your kids (biological and step) today will make an impact on them as adults. Hell, it will even make an impact on their future families.

All children respond differently to affection. My stepson, for example, will not leave the house without tracking me down for a hug, a kiss, and an I love you. My stepdaughter, on the other hand, is very much her father's daughter. Affection must be earned, and it's not given as freely. Still, when she and her sister cuddle up with me for a girls' night movie, she demands that I am in the middle so that I can cuddle with them both. These moments mean the world to me because it's these moments that serve as affirmation that I matter. Your presence matters to your stepchildren, and they love you even if they give and receive love differently. Look for every one of those little moments when someone else's child is willing and able to show you love. Appreciate those moments so that when times get tough again, you can remind yourself that you do matter.

You need to meet your stepchildren where they are when it comes to affection, but you must show up. If they resist, don't respond, pull back, or won't reciprocate, don't give up. Your relationship will grow if you find what works best for them, then make conscious efforts to show and tell them that you love them. Our own children take for granted that we love them. Our stepchildren, however, need constant confirmation that we do. Blending a family takes conscious endeavors to show love. Find, seek, and create ways to be connected to those babies who are not your biological children. Throw your arms around them when they come home, ask them how their weekend went, and tell them you love them whenever you can. It's your job to make them feel loved, not the other way around. Be the parent you needed when you were younger (no matter what your family dynamic looked like), and more than anything, be the parent you know they deserve.

THE BLENDED MANIFESTO

Love exists within every heart. The pathway to each heart, however, can look and feel different. Listen for the whispers. Keep an eye out for the snuggles, the smiles, the "sit-between-us" moments that let you know you matter in the lives of your blended family—littles and adults.

Generational Inheritance

(How hard it is to embrace everyone's personal histories)

Perhaps the most defining fact of my upbringing is that I grew up in the country with no running water. It's true, even though my husband didn't fully believe it until he finally worked up the courage to ask my mother during a margarita-enhanced lunch. When I say I grew up with no running water, that is not to say we didn't have water, it's just that for the first thirteen years of my life, water was more of a luxury item. Sometimes we had it, and sometimes we did not. You may be wondering how one's upbringing influences how many kids they have and how they raise their blended family . . . oh, it relates. Stay with me here; I'll explain.

When I was a child, my parents and I would load up in a 1950's rusted-out, two-ton international flatbed truck adorned with a 200-gallon green plastic water tank strapped down to the back, then drive twenty-five miles to a small north Texas town where we proceeded to drop quarters into a water machine much like an old car wash. A large water hose would fill up our tank until we ran out of quarters, and we would then haul our jackpot back home. There, we had a ramshackle pump house where we would pump the water from the green plastic water tank into a stainless-steel water tank, which was then piped into the double-wide trailer we lived in. When the water tank was empty, or when we ran out of quarters, or when the 1950's water hauler took a shit for a period of time, then we were out of water. I remember countless mornings when I only got a half glass of water, and that was all I had to brush my teeth with that day. Our water situation is also how I learned the art of bathing in just two inches of water or shampooing only the front half of my hair in the sink. If we were out of quarters, then we were out of water.

While I grew up with very little, my mother refused to call us poor. "No, baby," she would say, "we aren't poor, we're just broke." When I looked around and watched other kids at school, it felt like we were poor, but I was never allowed to use that term. My mother's distinction between "poor" and "broke" taught me something I wouldn't realize for many years to come: **Poor was a permanent condition; broke was temporary.** With her one constant linguistic correction, my mom was teaching me that I would get out of that place, that my present was not my future, that I was the only one who could determine what became of my life, and that I was in charge of my own success. Then and there a growth mindset began to form, one that would push me to constantly work my ass off and defy all the odds stacked against my success.

My biological children devour stories about me as a child and the kind of lifestyle I had. They hang on to every word when my mother shares stories with them. My daughter is obsessed with her familial background, much of which is dark and beyond what I want her to know at this point in her life. Still, my biological children see their own history in mine. It is simply not the same with my stepchildren. My biological children understand that my history is their shared history. They look at my parents as their familial lineage, a piece of their own identity, and it helps them understand where their mother came from and why she is the way she is—why she is money savvy, why she pushes to grow, get uncomfortable, and take on newer ventures and challenges, and why she had to develop grit and resilience.

For example, my son once asked me (well, yelled at me) as he was bemoaning the hardships of his life, "Mom, why are you always doing something? Why can't we ever just sit sometimes? Why is it always about getting things done? Why do you always have to be on me about getting everything done?" At the time, I yelled back something about get-your-ass-back-here-right-now-and-clean-this-shit-up. I wish I had been able to explain this story to him instead. I wish I had been more like my own mother who took all the time in the world to talk to me, to have conversations with me, to explain her *why* to me.

I am not that kind of mother. I am demanding and often unforgiving. And sometimes, many times in fact, I can be a lot harsher with my children as a result. Looking back, I gave more attention to my son's faults than his wins because, in my world, progress meant survival. My generational inheritance was that the world wasn't going to do him any favors, and it was my job to prepare him for that harsh reality. The sooner he learned, the better. Now, twenty-two years after becoming a mother, I am different in a lot of ways, but not in every way. I am still highly demanding, I expect my children to regularly contribute to the home, and them talking back is still a huge trigger for me. For better or for worse, our upbringing will always have a significant impact on our parenting. While our parenting will evolve over the years, to a certain extent we will default to our own childhood influences because that is all we knew as children, and it is what has been subconsciously embedded into our psyche. Unless we do the work to reconcile our past with our present and marry it with a compassionate understanding, we will forever be walking into present and future doors with the tattered and torn shoes of our past.

Parenting combines our past with our present. However, stepchildren do not share that same connection to a stepparent's personal history. And that's okay. Stepchildren will not be as invested in learning about your history because it is not a part of their history, which also means that they will not have as strong of an understanding about where you are coming from as a parent. My biological children learn the stories of my mother and my father, and it helps them understand why I can be so tough. It helps them understand why I push them so hard to succeed and why I can be unrelenting to a fault sometimes.

For my stepchildren, the same parenting style just leads to them feeling like they cannot ever please me, and that all I ever want to do is get them in trouble. My personal history simply does not translate to my stepchildren as an explanation for my parenting because it is not their history. It makes parenting harder, but it is okay. It's just another cultural difference found inside a blended family.

As stepparents, we must evaluate how our own past has influenced our current parenting and adjust accordingly. My expectations for my stepchildren, while coming from a place of love, were not being received as such because my history did not reflect their own. Similarly, you will likely need to adjust your expectations for your stepchildren, which is not to say you don't love them and want to show up for them in every way possible. In a way, a biological parent is better suited to carry the higher expectations for their own children because it can be balanced with the familial history and unconditional love children need to accept those higher expectations.

Without the connection to your personal history attached to your parenting style, your stepchildren may not understand that your expectations come from love. To them, your expectations can feel like unreasonable and unattainable requests aimed at catching them doing only bad things, fueling their belief that you do not love them as much as their biological parents. Your biological children may also feel the weight of high expectations from you, but their connection to your personal history helps them understand where you are coming from in a way your stepchildren may not understand.

Blending our personal histories into our newly created families creates unique challenges for the children of blended homes. My mother has been in my stepchildren's life since they were three and four years old, respectively. She has never missed giving a birthday or Christmas gift to any of our four children. My stepchildren call her Grandma Chris. She has attended their sporting events, babysat them on weekends so my husband and I could escape, and cooked meals with them. But her efforts do not replace the fact that she is a step-grandmother. My stepchildren will always have a tighter bond with their own mother's parents, and rightfully so, because that relationship is a part of their own personal history. My biological daughter idolizes my mother, and my mother lights up when they get a night for the two of them to make homemade pizzas and crepes. My daughter has a bond with my mother in a way my stepchildren do not, and my mother has a bond with my daughter in a way she does not with my stepchildren. And that's okay. My biological children deserve to have a close bond with my mother, just like my stepchildren do with their own grandparents.

My biological son has known my husband's parents since he was twelve years old. Both sides of my husband's family send him birthday cards, Christmas gifts, and show up for him whenever possible. Still, when my stepson got old enough to fly alone, he got the invitation to spend summer visits in California with my husband's mother, and my son did not. It hurt his feelings, and we talked about it. My husband's mother loves my son, and I know my son feels loved by her and her husband. Stepchildren just have a different relationship with grandparents versus step-grandparents. And again, that's okay.

In the same way a spouse is an in-law to their partner's family, so are stepchildren. While it hurts us as their parents for our children to feel left out, it is natural, and we must check our own biases and try to help our children understand the situation. It is simply another part of blended-family reality with which we must make peace. Making peace can be particularly difficult if your child is missing an entire side of their family tree due to an absentee parent, but that certainly doesn't mean there is a lack of love. It can make for uncomfortable family gatherings, but as hard as it is for us to maneuver our own blended family, our extended family members are also doing their absolute best as well.

In a blended family, we all begin as strangers. We all enter a brand-new circle of life that we are consciously creating—pasts and all. We accept that we must learn our spouse's past to fully understand who they are today. The same may be true for everyone your blended family has an impact on. It may help you to understand the family dynamic of your in-laws, your spouse's ex, or even your spouse's ex-wife's parents. Why not try to see why they are who they are and how their history has affected the stepchildren you are helping to raise? It may help to understand the generational background. Opening your heart to everyone's personal history is not to imply that it changes anything or makes everyone magically get along. It may, however, help you understand where these new people in your life are coming from. It may help you forgive when forgiveness is needed. It may help you admire something about a person you thought you could never care about. It may help you be compassionate and kind when it is hard to be so in the moments that make you feel as if you will spontaneously combust with that seething hot rage you feel. Embracing the personal histories of the people involved in your blended family is a first step in beginning to see everyone as real people.

THE BLENDED MANIFESTO

We each have our own unique histories that make their way into the blend that is our blended family. We need not pretend each other's personal history does not affect our family in current time. We don't have to be afraid to know each other and our personal histories. We don't have to be afraid to understand where someone is coming from.

CHAPTER 12

The Box Fan Rule

*(How hard it is to be in control of your
own feelings and responses)*

.

One morning my daughter came into my bathroom while I was getting ready, bawling that her sister—my stepdaughter—had hurt her feelings and called her gross. I talked her off the ledge, got her cleaned up, and sent her on her way. A bit later, as the family was gathering their things to leave for school, I spoke to my stepdaughter about how sometimes we say things to one another that may seem like no big deal, but they can still hurt the other's feelings. My stepdaughter immediately bristled up, yelled at me that she didn't do anything to *her*, and called my daughter a spoiled brat. I responded in a scream. I told her that my daughter was not a spoiled brat and that if anyone in this house was, it was the one who was always name-calling and bullying other people. I stormed out, my daughter left for school crying, both stepchildren left hating me, and my husband and I did not talk for the next two days. Talk about a bomb detonating and blowing everyone's emotions and feelings to smithereens.

I have to believe I am not alone in saying that this scenario happens a lot in blended families. It probably happens a lot in any family, but blended families carry their own distinct levels of hurt and name-calling, hitting, scratching, slapping, and, in general, siblings being assholes to each other. Since it is someone else's child inflicting all these pains onto your biological child, it's easy to get yourself in an amplified state of anger. Consider the last time one of your biological children smacked the crap out of their biological sibling, aka your other biological child. You might have gotten angry, and you might have laid down the law and corrected them for their misbehavior, but you were able to move on. *Because siblings will be siblings*, you tell yourself. Now think about the kid down the road, four years older than your child, slapping the crap out of your kid. How do you feel? Livid, I presume. The same applies in a blended-family scenario.

These are the types of situations blended families face daily. Of course I was pissed; I was more than pissed. Every time my daughter has been slapped, scratched, and hurt by my stepdaughter, it infuriates me to where I cannot control myself. If I am being real, I have smacked her back. I spanked her when she was younger because of these very behaviors. My husband, because both girls are his biological children, does not have near as an adverse reaction to our daughter getting bullied by her sister as I do. For one, he grew up with three siblings and the physical aggression between my husband and his brother is no joke. He has punished his children for being overly physical with our daughter, but only when I have let the entire house know, in a decibel level only dogs can hear, just how unacceptable these behaviors are. Thus, my stepchildren know I am the reason their dad is punishing them.

In a blended family, the picking of sides immediately ensues when an incident between children has occurred. Typically speaking, I rush to the defense of my biological daughter, and my husband's silence on the situation is a clear alliance with his biological kids. Only my daughter is *our* daughter, which, in turn, sends me into an ultra-high, 4K, def-com-red level of angry. I overcompensate by becoming overly protective of my daughter while being simultaneously furious at my husband for not coming to our daughter's defense. It's an exhausting way to live.

Blended families constantly pick sides. Intentional or not, our baggage and insecurities and our resentments and jealousies all find their way into the everyday fabric of blended-family dynamics. It's a fact—we pick sides.

It's not right, or maybe it is. I honestly do not know, but it is very much a reality. When I am being sane, I can see both sides of the story. Your children deserve your loyalty. They need to know you are going to stand up for them, take their side, keep anyone from harming them. The flip side is that parents cannot monitor every interaction between siblings, and part of the learning curve is figuring out how to handle all the other people with whom you have been thrown into this life.

On that particular morning, there was some serious side-picking happening. It was like a demented version of the game Red Rover, with our family lined up against each other, ready to brawl. Only none of the enemy lines were clear because my biological daughter was mine, but also his, and my stepchildren were his, but also my daughter's, and I was his, but also hers . . . and so goes the game of Red Rover: Blended Family Edition—the game where everyone loses!

The real problem on this particular morning, though, was not even about the name-calling stuff or the picking of sides. The real problem was that I had broken my own rule for myself. I had recently taken a private vow to stay out of morning family dynamics to the best of my ability. When all the kids were younger, staying out of the routine was not as viable of an option, as the mom is usually the one fixing lunches, signing folders, finding socks, tying shoes, and reviewing spelling words. But now that the kids are all older and mostly self-sufficient in the mornings, my presence started making things worse.

Once I recognized that the fifteen minutes before we all leave the house for school and work is a major trigger zone for our blend, I started taking steps to remove myself from the situation. I realized I could de-escalate our overall family dynamics by not being the one parenting all the shit in the mornings. Like clockwork, as soon as we are all gathering belongings around the kitchen table, someone says something to someone, someone else snaps back (whether it involved them or not), someone else corrects it, and another someone comments back until we all leave angry, hurt, or crying. Sometimes, all three. In response, I made two rules for myself to keep my feelings and reactions in check during the morning trigger time: 1) Turn the box fan on the highest level and stay in the bathroom, and 2) Do not parent or interfere with my husband's parenting, or lack thereof, even if it means not saying any words at all, on any given morning.

In an effort to minimize my own role in this toxic morning routine, I found that I'm always hot while getting ready anyway, and the box fan on high means I can't hear any of the BS happening in the other room. In short, *hear nothing; say nothing.* How glorious! By the time I get myself ready and join my family in the kitchen, I have yet to be influenced by what may or may not have been said or done before I arrived. My response to that morning's conflict, however, was a direct result of breaking the box fan rule. Given my second cardinal sin of stepping in as parent before 8:00 a.m., I only further escalated the situation.

The morning I broke my own rule, I doubled down. I didn't turn on the box fan, and I attempted to parent a situation between two children when I should have let my husband handle it . . . or not handle it, whichever the case may be. I had already done the triage portion of the morning. I had already talked to my daughter and calmed her down and helped her handle her feelings. I should have stopped there. My daughter would have been emotionally over it by the time she got to school, and everyone else would have gone about their day in peace. Instead, after she was okay, and during our trigger time, I attempted to parent my stepdaughter's choices about how she treated her sister. I called out my stepdaughter and addressed the situation in front of the entire family because I was angry. I wasn't even just angry about this incident. I was angry about all the other times I felt my daughter had been treated badly by her sister. But I should have stayed in my own lane because when I veered off, I only gave the behaviors power over us all, not the least of which was *me.*

In a blended family, any misstep may uncover a long-buried land mine ripe for explosion. As blended families, we are never in the present moment—we are living in a constant state of past wrongs and hurts squared up with our present and future. Thus, our instincts about how to react in any given situation cannot always be trusted, as our instincts are nearly always initially wrong when it comes to stepparenting. We can enter an encounter, thinking we are simply correcting a small behavioral issue, and before we know it, that bomb has exploded right in our faces. To support peace in our homes, we must create our own rules for engagement, and we must follow them.

The moment we lead without purpose, or attempt to prove a point, we will find our family covered in shrapnel, broken and torn apart. Whatever your rules for engagement are, whatever the trigger zones are for your blend (another big one for us is getting in and out of the car—what a shit show that one always is), put into place a policies-and-procedures manual for yourself. These personally imposed sanctions are as much for your family's sanity as they are for yours. Creating a few specific strategies to live by, day by day, will not only help your family dynamics but will keep you from wanting to beat the shit out of everyone in your home . . . er, I mean, help you be present and in control of your own reactions. Same thing, really.

When you break your own rules, and you frequently will, it will only solidify your need to honor the precautions you can take so you maintain composure and stay in control of yourself. As we are all trying to learn, that's the only thing you really have any control over in a blended family anyway.

...

You know that old saying, everyone makes mistakes? Well, I never learned that one. Modern parenting philosophy tells us that everyone makes mistakes, but the important thing is to let our children know that it is not the end of the world, which I never did very well with the parenting of any of our four children. In hindsight, I should have. My son, being the oldest child, primarily took the brunt of my overbearing and demanding parenting style. In my world, mistakes were a margin of error that could send everything I had worked so hard for into the shitter in an instant. Just like that, one mistake could critically throw off the path of success. The electricity would get turned off because a ticket obliterated my monthly budget, a missed deadline meant my financial aid would not arrive for an entire semester, and an absent signature on a day care assistance renewal application meant I couldn't afford childcare. Whatever the mistake was, the consequences seemed so huge that I learned to fear mistakes. I was (and still am in large part) terrified of making mistakes. I have cried over some spilled milk in my day, y'all. When you fear making a mistake, you begin the downward spiral of controlling everyone and everything around you.

For years my parenting style was directly rooted in control: control of situations, control of the past, control of the future, control in anything and everything because if I was not in control, then my life felt out of control. Even when my son was a young child, I showed little tolerance for his tantrums, emotional breakdowns, or personal challenges. The life stresses I faced when he was younger did not allow me to have the patience with him that he needed and deserved. He internalized my own fear of mistakes and is now working through his own versions of perfectionism and control issues. Nothing like inheriting a lifelong obsession with you'll-never-be-good-enough. I am so sorry about that one, honey.

When I became a stepmother, I believed that the only way to show my stepchildren I loved them was to treat them just like I had my own child. Only my stepchildren did not have the history with me, they did not have the same parental bond with me, and I had not been caring for them since the day they were born. Becoming a stepmother shed the first bit of light on my own parenting inadequacies. My parenting toolbox no longer worked, and I was not super excited to admit how much of my parenting tactics needed an overhaul. It would be many years before I truly reevaluated the harshness with which I parented and the level of expectations I had placed on all four of our children. My personal history played an enormous role in the evolution of my own parenting. The more I healed myself from trauma and wounds, the better parent and stepparent I became.

When we look closely, there is almost always a connection between how we parent and how we were parented. As a result, we are either striving to do the very same or striving to do something completely different. Either way, there is no win. At some point we all must learn how to be the best parent *we* can be, and not because of, or in spite of, anyone else's parenting that came before us. If you had the most amazing, kind, patient, and mature parents the world has ever known, then the pressure to be that same parent is a very real thing. If you had demanding parents with strict expectations and swift consequences, then you are likely swinging the pendulum in a completely different direction or repeating much of the same behavior.

The moral of the story is to let your children make mistakes. Let your stepchildren make mistakes. Let your spouse make mistakes. Truthfully, even let your spouse's ex make mistakes. Let yourself make mistakes. The growth of your blended family is directly correlated to your personal growth. And so is the health of your marriage as well as your relationship with your children and stepchildren. Yes, even your relationship with your spouse's ex. I hear it all the time . . . "His ex is so high conflict" or "My child's father only wants to control me" or "These kids are not taught respect and manners." Insert your personal bitch-fest here, then take a good long look at yourself and start making the changes that only you can make because the only thing you should be controlling is *your response* to *your world*, especially when your blended family turns into a shit show. And it will absolutely turn into a shit show at times. And that's okay.

...

Over the last few years, I have been trying to evolve from being someone who reacts to all situations immediately to someone who can sit back and process feelings before responding. One of my favorite women in Hollywood, Whitney Cummings, says that when discussing control issues, "Wait for the urgency to lift before responding."[3] Weakening the reaction mechanisms in my brain has become my personal obsession, and it's still only going so-so.

During an especially tough season in our family (which, quite frankly, we are still in with two teenagers in the home), I picked up a book by Ryan Holiday and Stephen Hanselman called *The Daily Stoic: 366 Meditations on Wisdom, Perseverance, and the Art of Living.* This book kept my soul afloat when I thought my head would explode. It calmed me the fuck down. The premise of the book is not about stepparenting or blending families, or even parenting for that matter. The concept is about taking back the original meaning of the word "stoicism"—moving the term from its present understanding of being aloof, distant, and devoid of emotions to the original meaning of simply being in control of one's own feelings and actions.

The true version of the word eluded me. I am forever popping off, saying out loud what everyone else is comfortable just thinking, stepping on toes, sometimes insulting people, and frequently pissing them off. Stoicism, or having control over my own feelings and reactions, was a mind-blowing concept for me. Still is. The practice of not allowing anyone else to fluster me, pull my triggers, or make me lose control of *myself* felt particularly powerful as a strategy in maneuvering through our blended-family days. Control of our surroundings, even our days, is hard to come by in a blended world. Our daily schedules, our dinnertime routines, our household responsibilities, our expectations . . . it frequently feels like we have no control over any of it. Except we do—over ourselves and how we show up in each moment, even the explosive ones.

A lack of control is a recurring theme in blended homes. The lack of control can easily lead to a grasping for control, which leads to a lot of controlling tendencies. And it's the same for everyone. In so many blends I know, everyone is grasping for their portion of the control in the family. Stepchildren, biological parents, stepparents, biological kids, half siblings, full siblings—all vying for the control they need to feel secure, seen, heard, and loved.

I have felt restrained in so many instances, believing I had little ability to create change. The problem was, however, that I was looking to create change for everyone around me instead of for myself. *If I could just make everyone else see what I see, we would be healthier. If I could just be what every single person needs, every time they need it. If I could just figure out the right way to handle every single scenario, then I could fix everyone.* Big reveal . . . I couldn't. I only caused more strife when I tried to "help" everyone, when I tried to "teach" everyone, when I tried to "push" everyone. If people want those things, they will go get them for themselves. If they wanted my help in any way, they would ask for it, and I would gladly offer it! Breaking yourself down because you believe that you alone have the power to fix it all is simply unsustainable. You're setting yourself up to fail, my friend. We end up feeling like everything is done to us, personally and intentionally, ultimately resulting in convincing ourselves we have little power to change anything at all. The truth is that you can only change *you*. It's simple and unsexy, I know. It's the granny panties you go to when you eat too much pizza. It's the age-old truth—you really only have control over yourself. I know that now. Mostly.

Stoicism brought to light for me the impact controlling one's self can have on our blended lives. Not only does it keep me from saying and doing a lot of things that I only regret and carry guilt for later, but it makes my family feel more loved. Stoicism, the true meaning of the word, has allowed me to become more aware of the control I have over myself, which has greatly affected the level of content in my life.

Mothers, especially, tend to have control issues in their families. We believe that if we can just plan for everything, if we can just communicate flawlessly, if we can just control our surroundings, then we can make our families better. These beliefs always backfire. Embracing the idea of stoicism brought to light, for me, what should have been painfully obvious. I can only control my own feelings and reactions. Period. I can only control myself. Yes, I hear you, you fellow control freaks out there who think I'm full of shit right now. Clearly, I don't know how well you plan and schedule and communicate and control . . . er, I mean guide and parent and handle and manage. Insert all the other words you fancy yourself doing, but the bottom line is control.

The cold, hard truth is that in a blended family, amidst a complete lack of control, we very often double down. We grasp control over more of everything and everyone because we know we actually have no control over any of it. The cycle of control tells us that when our control tactics (and they are control tactics) no longer work, it must mean we just need more control. So, we plan and schedule and communicate and *control* some more. The cycle continues until our children are miserable, our marriage is busted, and we feel like failures because we were so invested in the belief that we can fix everything for everyone. Shit, haven't you realized by now that not only can you not "fix" anyone else, they may not actually need to be "fixed"?

While I certainly have not mastered the concept of stoicism, I have accepted it into my life like some accept Jesus into their heart at the altar. That said, I do stumble, and I do fail at times. I lose the battle with myself so effin' often. But I have a guide now. I have a belief to fall back on. Stoicism rejects the belief that we can, or should, be in control of anything but ourselves. That doesn't mean anything but ourselves, our children, our spouse, and our spouse's ex. Nope. It means we can only be in control of *ourselves*. Now, when I see the cracks in our blend, I do not have to assume the entire fault or responsibility for creating them and patching them. There is true freedom in relinquishing control. Giving up control of others leaves space to gain control of yourself. I have freed up my mind to think about other things.

I have freed up my soul to work on me. And doing so has made my family more open to hearing what I have to say, when I truly have something to say.

THE BLENDED MANIFESTO

Mistakes are a part of every relationship. There is no such thing as perfect, just progress. Accept that progress is something you cannot control. Not everyone else's anyway, just your own. So, how can you find your blend of stoicism in your life? What would that look like? What would that feel like, for you? Nobody else, just yourself? Who would you be? What would you think/do/be? Chew on that for a hot second.

CHAPTER 13

The Backfire

(How hard it is to learn you don't know it all)

For years I was the primary disciplinarian in our home. I was the primary parent to my stepchildren 50 percent of the time and to my biological children 100 percent of the time. Even with my shared daughter, I carried the bulk of the parenting responsibility. It is a trap I believe most mothers and stepmothers can relate to having. I handled drop-offs, pickups, dinner, cleaning, homework, medications, sports, and the multiple life schedules that existed in our home. I assigned chores, handled the rewards and consequences, and made sure lunches were made and clothes were washed. In short, I did all the shit work no one else wanted to do. Being the primary parent to your children is hard. Being the primary parent to stepchildren will backfire on your ass quicker than you can say get me the fuck outta here.

To be clear, I'm not saying my husband isn't a present and loving father. Not at all. It's just that becoming the primary caregiver is easy trap for women to fall into because as women, especially those who are already mothers, we often don't even notice we've picked up the bulk of the child-raising responsibilities . . . until about a decade later when we wake up one day mad as shit about it. But heed my warning: The early habits you allow your marriage to fall into are the very habits the foundation of your marriage will be built upon. Suffice it to say, if you start doing significantly more of the work now, it will take an exorcism of all family members to get your ass out of it later. Pay attention to the habits in the first three years of your blending family. They will matter ten years down the road.

My husband, a newly single man, married me, a woman who had been mothering on her own for thirteen years. He had toddlers; I had a teenager. He had not parented alone; I had only done it alone. He had divorced-parent guilt; I had systems in place and expectations set and not an ounce of parental guilt because I had been on my own with my child since I was seventeen. I suspect some part of that was comforting to him. He had only been a parent a few years and had been only recently thrown into it on his own. When we blended our lives, my need for control plus his lack of experience were the perfect ingredients for the resentment martini soon to come.

When we blended, I had a strict and specific bedtime routine; he had them watch movies until they fell asleep. I had chore charts and report card expectations; he had toddlers who could not reach the sink. I had a specific daily plan for picking up and cleaning up after ourselves around the house; he couldn't care less if things were left lying around. I had a chip on my shoulder; he had not yet been given the opportunity to figure out what his ways were going to be. I was confident my way was the right way. Thus, I projected confidence that I knew best, and he let me run with it. Did some structure need to happen? Yes, absolutely. Toddlers will run wild over a home with no structure. But I didn't need to be the one enforcing the structure. In all honesty, I only knew what worked for my son and me. And in hindsight, who is to say it even "worked" for my son and me given that I now think I was way too hard on him during his childhood. My expectations were too high for myself, and that bled into my parenting.

My personal circumstances dictated that I have structure and control in an effort to keep it all together. My husband's circumstances differed vastly. He only had his children 50 percent of their life. His two toddlers had just been dragged through the mud in an ugly divorce and custody battle. His children were not even school-aged yet. My assertion of how his children needed to be raised was just that—my assertion. Thus, our blended-family dynamics evolved in such a way that I controlled how most of the child-rearing happened. Our mutually accepted family dynamic worked, until it didn't.

Children generally accept discipline and behavior expectations well into grade school. As those school-aged children become preteens and teenagers, however, their desire to please begins to dissipate, and those sweet little tub-of-loves are replaced with irate, talking-back, eating, crying, emotional gobstoppers. Our family arrangement of me setting and enforcing household expectations slowly began to crumble around us all. The older my husband's children got, the more I expected of them, and my level of expectation began to differ greatly from my husband's expectations of his own children.

It is easier for parents to back each other up when the kids are young and the expectations are things like take your medicine, bathe regularly, and be in bed on time (although we fought quite a bit about those things as well). As children get older, their ability to contribute to the home should increase. The expectations evolve based on their ability to do more for themselves and others. As the children in our home aged, my husband had more parenting under his belt and therefore had opinions of his own about whether he supported my expectations of his children. He had ideas about his children having chores, cleaning up after themselves, and contributing to the upkeep of the home. Quite frankly, we still frequently disagree about these things.

I realized that even though I had been leading the child-rearing did not mean I would continue in this role. My husband was still on his own parenting journey. I had to start making peace with the fact that just because I believed my way was the right way to raise kids did not mean my husband would agree. We began to clash, heavily. My husband suddenly began disagreeing with and calling out my parenting of his children, specifically. I was still the lead parent when it came to my own biological son and daughter, but the household dynamic was shifting when it came to my stepchildren. The open arguments about expectations and enforcement began suffocating our home. My kids felt like our world revolved around my stepchildren, and my stepchildren felt like everything wrong with our family was their fault.

Screaming matches about our children were occurring in front of our children regularly. Our marriage was suffering, and so were our children. My stepchildren became defiant when I asked them to do anything, and I became angry when I felt disrespected as the mother in our home who took care of everything for everyone. My husband felt like he was constantly picking sides and defending his children. By then I had a teenager and a five-year-old who felt resentful that their expectations were significantly higher than those for the other children in the home. My daughter started asking me questions as to why her brother and sister were allowed to act in ways she was not. Our blend was breaking. There were cracks in our foundation, and I could not understand why, after all the work we had done to blend our dynamics, something so beautiful was falling apart.

Looking back, I can clearly see that the backfire came from me assuming the primary parental role with my stepchildren years previously, and from my husband's expectation for me to do so. Neither of us had any idea we would end up resenting the hell out of each other years later. Life does not afford us the luxury of knowing now what we didn't know then. The kicker is that you will still have to pay for the shit you didn't even know you were doing. And we were most definitely paying. I was paying him back for how he treated my son, he was paying me back for setting the bar too high for his children, and our children were paying us back for the inconsistencies in their lives. Payback is a bitch, and she doesn't go away on her own. We had to come together to extract the anger from our home, and it still comes up, a lot.

The backfire of a blended family is when marriages begin to break, when couples go to bed alone and wake up angry. Blended families work in cycles. A couple may work through the current stage of funk in their marriage with the belief that once handled, they can wipe their hands of that problem and move on down the road. Only it doesn't work that way for us. The same problems keep coming up, over and over again. They may present themselves in different scenarios, but the same problems just keep reappearing in new forms. I always compare blended-family life to the game of Whac-A-Mole we played as kids. Just when you hit one mole, another one pops up, and you often find yourself having to hit many at one time. Our marital problems in a blended family are just like that game. Just as you smash one down, another one (or three) pops up.

Something to consider: Most of us in blended families already have at least one failed relationship in our past—at least one marriage or partnership that did not work. Are we simply living a slightly better version of the same problems that cursed us before? What did we learn from that previous failed relationship? Did we learn the power of vulnerability, to know what needs to be said and what doesn't, or how to see the world through someone else's perspective? Not really. That relationship ended, after all. It didn't get better or didn't seem like it could get better, so it ended. That's what happens to marriages that don't learn and grow and get better. They end. Just a generation ago, the typical expectation was that couples made marriages work no matter how bad they got, but making a marriage work forever isn't our sociocultural standard anymore. Keeping the marriage intact is not the only acceptable option for the modern-day family. Today, it is more important to maintain the overall health and well-being of all parties involved. Choosing one's peace and happiness takes priority over choosing to stay in an ideal set by traditional society. Today, people break up, marriages end, and for the most part, our society accepts separation as a healthy, viable option. We have a looser cultural acceptance for giving up on a marriage and ending a family. And rightfully so, mostly.

The odds are certainly stacked against us in blended families. Lose a first family, and the scars run deep. Lose a second family, and they may never fully heal. We are maneuvering partnerships that innately involve significantly more conflict, jealousy, resentments, competition, and double standards, and we are doing it while likely managing much tougher life issues than in the first marriage because so many more hearts are involved the second or third time around. Some days it can feel like an impossible mountain to climb. With all the dynamics already stacked against us, combined with all the things we never fully figured out about making a marriage work in the first place, our blended-family success rate is scary low. And often not for a lack of love or desire but rather a lack of awareness around the world about what our families face. We all think it's just us. Just our home. Just our marriage. Just our blend handling the chaos, hurt, and loneliness. We go through highs of being utterly in love with our families to bouts of despair when questioning whether we made the right decision.

Pulling the trigger and walking away from a marriage or long-term relationship when children are involved is gut-wrenching. My own marriage is not immune. We have had moments of staring down the barrel of quitting. We have not actually quit, but we have had occasions when it felt like we were causing more harm than good for everyone involved. These moments are intense, and personal, and crippling. When days turn into weeks or months of disconnect, when your home feels like it is housing two families instead of one, when you cannot think of how to turn the ship around, and when you feel like you have done everything you can do, in these moments I say to you, get help and give it one more day. Then get some more help and give it a few more days. Finally, get more help and give it a month. The odds that any one person in a marriage can change that relationship with only the tools they picked up thus far is a Hail Mary. It could work, or it could not. But it is your marriage you are taking that chance on, and your family that will pay the price if it doesn't work.

There are many ways of getting help. It can come in the form of dinner with a close friend who may be willing to help you remember why you started your family in the first place. It can be making a counseling appointment or going on a long walk alone or with your spouse. It can be signing yourself up for a pottery class or a Sip and Paint with friends. Getting help can look like spending two hours in the self-help section of the local bookstore or asking your spouse to handle dinner for the kids so you can go out to a restaurant alone to collect your thoughts. Getting help is just the conscious process of making yourself better so that you can then show up better for yourself, your family, and your partner. But it does not happen quickly. I would argue that it takes at least a year to get real with a counselor about what's happening in your home and your marriage, and maybe another full year to implement change. But if you don't do it, if you don't find a way to get help that creates real change for yourself, your marriage and family are at a higher risk of ending.

Now, the flip side. Getting help is not calling your best friend to vent all your frustrations about your spouse, your kids, or the ex in your life. That's just venting. Getting help does not equal airing out sensitive information or dirty laundry with just about anyone. You may still need to vent but do recognize that venting is not getting help or creating change in yourself and your marriage. Venting just validates and justifies you to create more of the same behaviors. And remember that what you focus on is what grows. You likely do not walk away from a venting session with a heart that is more open or looking to forgive and compromise. We walk away from a venting session armed and dangerous, looking to prove some shit. I did it for years, and I still find myself getting caught up in the trap of venting. We may not rid ourselves of it completely but start entertaining the idea that venting isn't creating any real change for you or your family.

Getting help is also not about having a mommy's night out with so much wine that you hurt the next morning or stopping for happy hour after work and then showing up late at home in a drunken stupor. Again, you may still need these outings but recognize that they are not helping create change in yourself and your marriage. These types of actions most definitely only add problems and increase the likelihood of your marriage and family ending.

Some people in blended families have turned to alcohol to numb the problems facing them at home, but this behavior only teaches children to do the same and further harms marriages.

It is hard work to keep a blended family together, to sail through the rough, uncharted waters that come with each person and their unique personality in your blend. It is especially difficult when no one can be open enough to admit the specifics of what the family is going through behind closed doors. We have already established that we are just a hot mess to begin with, a couple of louts who probably didn't do the inner work they needed to before they jumped into creating a family all over again. It does not mean our marriages cannot thrive. Take having an infection, for example. If we wake up with strep throat one morning, we can go to the doctor. We can get a steroid shot and an antibiotic to help clear up the infection. If we go on the first day we feel sick, we can be healthy and back on our feet in no time. If we don't go, if we avoid the doctor's office, if we wait it out for a few days with the belief that we can fix ourselves, we've not only infected our entire family, but we've only made ourselves sicker. When your marriage gets sick, if one or both people involved get an infection and won't get treated, won't get help, the virus may pass. It may work itself out in time. It just will likely get much worse than it has to, and it may make you much sicker than need be. So quit the whining and start becoming intentional with your blend and how you approach the challenges you face together.

THE BLENDED MANIFESTO

It's okay to admit that this is hard work. It is work that isn't often rewarded or seen right away, yet its effects are felt almost immediately and last decades. It's okay to relinquish control of everything and everyone else. The only one you can really parent or re-parent is yourself. From there, all change and growth take place.

CHAPTER 14

A Decade Later

(How hard it is to remember how far we have all come)

Here we are, ten years later. Our family is bonded, mostly happy, and a handful for anyone to handle. When all six of us are home, it gets just as loud as it did when the kids were little, running around and shooting Nerf guns in our faces. And sometimes, when all six of us are home, we are still running around and shooting Nerf guns in each other's faces. Our family feels stable. It's our very own blend of stability. I'm not here to pretend that we've learned all our lessons and know what we are doing now. In fact, I think our success is just the opposite. We have learned that we have no idea what we are doing. We have learned that it's okay to mess it all up. We have learned that our children will be okay if our marriage is okay. We have a young man embracing adulthood, two teenagers coming up on driving so much faster than I am prepared for, and a young girl maturing by leaps and bounds. We haven't mastered shit, we have just learned the significance of accepting and embracing each person in our family, as fully as humanly possible, in that exact moment in time.

My son and my husband have forged a bond that has truly helped heal their hearts. They needed each other. My son needed a man to step in and become his father. He needed to have proof that a dad can stick around and show love. He needed what I could never give him—a guide for how to become a man. My husband needed the opportunity to face his own demons in order to heal from some of his own childhood traumas by being the kind of stepfather he didn't have. My husband has dug deep to build his bond with my son, excavating feelings he would rather have left dead and buried. Today, they call and text each other and have a relationship completely independent of me. They are father and son.

While I am still maneuvering through being a stepmom to two teenagers, I now know parenting your stepchildren "just like you would your own children" is the kiss of death. Is it stupidly hard to know how to parent one child while simultaneously stepparenting another? Absofuckinglutely. But you have to figure it out. What feels like strict and loving parenting to my biological children feels like being called out and unwanted to my stepchildren. I still have expectations and boundaries for them, but they have changed drastically. I am getting better at replacing parenting them with just loving them, as often as I can. If there is a situation I can walk away from and not parent or say whatever is inside my head, I try to do so. Sometimes, I am successful. And in those moments where my own precautions fail and I overstep my boundaries, I give myself grace, and the kids as well.

The season we are in today is a more experienced one. We are more mindful and more forgiving. We have family struggles to work through, and we still differ a great deal on how to handle them. We often disagree about chores, responsibilities, and grades. I still struggle to check my own resentments about how my son was raised versus how my stepchildren are being raised. We struggle to raise the "our baby" in the midst of double standards, and the bulk of the responsibility of raising her often falls to me.

The thing about blended families is that they are ever evolving in massively disruptive ways. Our life changes do not stem from positive events—if life is going well in a blended family, I assure you that no one wants to change it. As blended families, we are forever working through the hard stuff. When my fifteen-year-old stepson came to live with us full time two years ago, it was not out of the kindness of his mother's heart or because he was ready to make that life decision. He came to live with us full time because of struggles at his mother's house and because he was not succeeding and hadn't been for some time. His mother had not been ready to see him go at thirteen. Both houses tried everything they knew to do.

Conflict was driving a wedge between my stepson and his mother, and his sister was often caught in the crossfire. In blended families, conflict is a very real hurdle, one that we as parents do not usually handle well. His mother wasn't happy to see him move in with his father full time, and it still takes a toll on our relationships. What no one tells you before you get into a blended family is the obvious: that the kids keep growing. The kids keep getting older, and they keep needing different things from different people. Ultimately, my stepson needed his father full time. It was not an easy decision for anyone, especially my stepson.

...

Today, my marriage is mostly in a good place. We even managed to go to Las Vegas together for three days without having one fight or argument. My husband is my favorite travel companion, but if you have ever been to Vegas with a spouse and not ended up in a fight—well, it's pretty much the Holy Grail of marriage. The first time we went to Vegas together was more like the "two stooges" of marriage. We had grandiose ideas of the perfect Vegas getaway, only our versions of that perfect getaway did not match up. I thought we would walk the Strip, hand in hand, and have brunch on a patio with bottomless mimosas while overlooking the action of the city. My husband's version of Vegas was not leaving the casino except for a round of golf. Basically, I was looking for the girls' weekend version of Vegas, and he was looking to hit twenty-one. The result? Too much wine, getting utterly lost in the casino, and cussing out my husband in the hotel room once I finally found it.

The beginning of our blend was similar. We had two different versions of how our family should look. We did not know how to talk to each other, how to respect each other, or how to love each other the way the other person needed. That last one is still hard some days. Our expectations were unattainable, and we thought that by lowering them, we were also lowering our standards. We confused happiness with perfection, and perfection does not exist in any family, much less a blended family. When the stakes are so high, and you have already dragged your children through so much, the pressure we often put on our blended families is insurmountable. It is easy to end up feeling like everything is a huge mistake, and we ask ourselves, "What have we gotten ourselves and our kids into?" Keep remembering that no matter the work you put into your family, if you aren't matching the work you are putting into yourself, happiness will elude you, your spouse, and the children involved.

Fast-forward five years in our marriage. Our second trip to Las Vegas could not have been more different. My husband still wanted to gamble into the morning hours, and I still wanted to watch the lights from our room while ordering room service and watching overly priced pay-per-view. Ladies, you know there is nothing better than a hotel suite, room service, and a new release. So that is what we did. We allowed each other the freedom to do what we wanted, and we met each other halfway in the process. I found electronic roulette, which is my version of gambling without the obnoxious pressure of people around you at a roulette table yelling "hit on red" or whatever it is that people scream out. When I was done losing my money and maintaining my resting bitch face so nasty men wouldn't talk to me, I went back to the room. And that was okay. We spent one night together at a Cirque du Soleil show and a fancy dinner, and we balanced what each of us wanted and needed. The difference between the outcomes of our first trip to Vegas together and our second? A lot of personal growth and forgiveness.

A decade of learning about each other, accepting each other's faults, forgiving each other's failures, and being willing to lower our expectations has dramatically decreased the conflict in our home. Much too often, the adults leading blended families confuse lowering their expectations with settling, and I was guilty of that for years. They are not interchangeable concepts. Lowering your expectations in a blended family simply means acknowledging what everyone has been through and cutting everyone a little slack in their own journey to get where you think they should all be. It also means you learn to cut yourself some slack. You do not have to be the perfect one in the family, juggling everybody's everything forever. Let some plates fall; let them shatter at your feet. Let your expectations of what you think everyone *should be* shatter with them, yourself included. Accept the imperfection of your family and yourself. Disengage when necessary and re-engage whenever possible. Forgive yourself, forgive your family members, and forgive ex-spouses. Wherever you have taken on too much of the responsibility, let go of some things. Trust in your family to pick up the pieces for you but also remember that if you never let go of anything, they won't ever be able to help you. And when they don't, because sometimes they just won't, talk to your counselor to see if it is something you even need to spend energy on. Don't try to do it all alone, and don't expect anyone around you to know what you need because that's for you to figure out for yourself. Family should be there to love and support you, but don't confuse love and support with doing the inner work you have to do for yourself. No one is given a free pass from doing the inner work, and therein lies the most crucial ingredient in creating your unique blend and allowing it to mature over the years.

THE BLENDED MANIFESTO

Let acceptance and surrender be the guiding path for your blended journey. Surrender brings with it a lot of power and grace. Dance with the imperfections and put down the sword you are carrying— everything that happens is not your responsibility. Most of all, remember we are all growing and learning at our own pace. Give credit where credit is due and be honest with yourself about when that credit it due.

CHAPTER 15

Seeing in 3D

(How hard it is to see the human in each other)

My mom brain worries incessantly about the safety of my kids. I worry no less than eight times a day that my children will die, like every time they go outside, anytime they are out of sight, or when I don't know where they are for any period of time. And don't get me started on the anxiety over a grown child moving out on their own. I'm pretty sure I didn't sleep the first two years my son had his own apartment. Maybe it's a by-product of being an '80's baby—a generation of latchkey kids who came home after school and watched Oprah and the news (because cable wasn't much of a thing yet), witnessed every atrocity of the decade on live television, and sometimes even in our elementary school classrooms. Or maybe it was my own overly protective mother and father who forever prepared me for everything that could happen, and all the things that could go wrong. Whatever the reasons, the world has always felt like a dangerous place to me. It's as if we exist in a real-life Hunger Games—sending my children out into the world feels like facing certain death.

I struggle with something I like to call "overprotective mothering." I frequently talk myself off ledges just to muster up the courage to allow my daughter to play alone in the backyard. I come from a generation of girls who remember the kidnappings of Elizabeth Smart and Jaycee Dugard, and so many more who never came home. As a result, my mind can be hijacked by fear. As I sit writing this very paragraph, my mama mind is typing words while simultaneously counting the seconds that go by that I don't hear my daughter's voice in the backyard—in our fenced-in backyard with three dogs in it. I often struggle to get any work done when half my mind is focused on the fear that my daughter will get snatched up if I leave her alone for any amount of time.

When I give in to my fears and go check on her, she happily tells me she's "helping the chickens catch bugs." I exhale. She is alive. She has not been kidnapped only to be sold into sex trafficking. I can breathe again and go back to work for ten more minutes. It's funny, but it's not. It is an anxious way to live life. As parents, so much of our mind is reserved for our children that there is sometimes little space left for anything else that matters to us. As Leisse Wilcox explains in her book, *To Call Myself Beloved*, "like a vine out of control, our mind can be ravaged and taken over by anxiety and fear."[4] I find this sentiment to be especially true in a blended family where emotions run deep and history runs short.

We need to conscientiously maintain the vine inside our heads, keeping it lush, hearty, and in check. If we stop tending to the vine, it will grow and attach itself around the crevasses, hijacking our ability to see the forest for the trees. When our minds are taken over with anxious thoughts, we can no longer see our circumstances through a clear lens. We begin creating the story we are telling ourselves about the people around us because we've lost the ability to be open and honest with ourselves.

"Anxiety" was not a word I ever used to describe what I was feeling, but I have come to appreciate that that's exactly what it is. Anxiety looks like overprotective mothering, fighting with loved ones in the mirror, or losing complete control of your temper. It looks like planning for the next thirty years instead of the next four hours. It looks like stalking the ex-wife on social media in some derailed attempt at proving your own worth or jumping to conclusions and hitting send on that group text to your husband and the step-wife, letting them know exactly what you think of their last parenting decision. I have certainly had foot-in-the-mouth syndrome enough times to know. Anxiety can even look like control disguised as helping or your classic case of self-martyrdom—that need to do everything for everyone while running yourself ragged because you just cannot let go of control. That vine will take over if we are not vigilant in our own personal growth.

Personal growth in a blended family is a must. Our families tend to move at a wicked-fast speed as it is. If we, as the leaders of these families, are not evolving on our own journey, then we are not teaching our children how to evolve, yet we expect the children to grow and mature. Although we are their primary role models, we have resisted challenging ourselves to grow and mature. If we don't exemplify what we want and envision for our children, they will not follow suit. Children, no matter your family situation, do as you do, not as you say. If the relationships in our blended families have not advanced over the years, we really need to be willing to see our own contributions to the chaos. The disrespect. The distrust. The empathy. The forgiveness. The lack thereof.

In order to create a bond in your family, to create a home your children come back to as adults, you must be able to see others in 3D. The multifaceted view. All too often we prefer the one-dimensional version of the humans with whom we interact. We would rather see the face value of a person that supports the narrative we have created inside our heads—that version of the other person we have latched on to, that version that makes us feel better about ourselves. We rarely acknowledge the humanness or diverse makeup of the person that most likely would challenge the narrative we have built up in our minds about them.

Molding the family you say you want requires tearing up the picture you have of them and allowing a three-dimensional person to appear. Whether it is a relationship with your ex, your spouse's ex, or a stepchild, the relationship will not advance until you see the other person as a multidimensional, multi-layered human being.

Lovely, you must be thinking right about now. *That is just absofuckinglutely lovely, but how in the hell do you do it? How do you change the image you have in your head of another person? How do you forgive and release anger you still feel justified to carry? How do you remember to regularly lead with love and grace instead of insecurities and fears? How do you recognize the role control plays in your life?* I do have the answers, but you probably won't like them. It requires work. Time. Showing kindness when you don't want to. Critiquing your own contribution to a situation before critiquing anyone else's. Retraining your brain. Ultimately, accepting that your mind needs some rewiring. It's not rocket science, it's just a very intentional way of living. And the only way you can rewire your neural pathways and shift the way you think, the way you behave, or even the language you choose to use is by tapping into your subconscious and understanding where your own fears, insecurities, and hang-ups stem from originally. Once you understand that, it's time to feel into what you would like to create—in this case, the family that you say you want and desire. And once you're absofuckinglutely clear on how you want that to feel, tap into who each person is—their whole three-dimensional self—and give them grace. Be the one who sees possibilities instead of lia-bilities. Be the one who dives inward first before pointing fingers elsewhere, the one who can calm their mind and collect their emotions without feeling the pressure to resolve everything in the moment it is taking place. Be the one who starts peeling back the layers of each individual in your blend, so together y'all can create your own blend, shape new layers, and create new pathways for each other.

THE BLENDED MANIFESTO

Think of your blend as a tray of nachos layered with chips, salsa,
spicy peppers, and cheese. Each layer is messy, but once you dive in
and allow yourself to taste it fully, the outcome is delicious. Blended
families work a similar way. In order to understand yourself and your
blend, you gotta peel back the layers and keep going.

CHAPTER 16

The Answers to the Test

(How hard it is to implement the change we know we need)

Since we often just want someone to give us the answers to the test, here are the answers to the most common conflicts blended families regularly face. Now, please understand that I am not claiming that I do all of these things, I am just telling you what you *should* do in each of the scenarios. To actually implement any of them, you will have to retrain your brain to do so. It is going to take some genuine effort to create the mindset that allows you to change your responses in any given situation. It's like someone giving you the answers but not telling you which test question each answer belongs to. Even with a cheat sheet, you still have to do the work for the answers to matter. Having prefaced that, here you go!

My stepchild talks back to me. How should I respond?

It depends. If your stepchild is only in your home 20 percent of the time (your basic every-other-weekend custody arrangement), you should ignore it. Always. If you are only in this child's life roughly 20 percent of the time or less, then expecting change in this particular behavior is like wishing on a shooting star. You can do it if it makes you feel better, but that star doesn't give a shit about your behavioral expectations. And maybe it shouldn't. Our stepchildren are going through some shit too. Maybe the weekends your stepchild is with your spouse are the best weekends for you to go visit family, see friends, take your biological children to do something special, or leave everyone at home and take a day trip by yourself. Whatever you do, give your spouse and stepchild some time alone together. If you have a stepchild in your life 20 percent of the time or less, please take a back seat during that time and start retraining your brain to step back without anger or resentment. It will help the relationships grow in the long run.

If you have a stepchild talking back to you who is in the home 20 percent of the time or less while you, the stepparent, is the one managing most of the parenting, this question becomes tougher. Now you are the one doing the parenting while also getting talked back to. In this case, stop doing the parenting. I know. That seems impossible and unrealistic. It's not. It's tough enough for a biological parent to be taken seriously as a parent, a stepparent may never be. During those weekends, do not act as the primary parent to the stepchild. Expect your spouse to handle it.

If you have your stepchild 50 percent or more of their life, this question becomes much trickier. If your stepchildren are in the home most of the time, it's highly likely that the stepmom is doing a lot for everyone, including the bulk of the parenting and the managing of the house. If a stepchild is talking back to the stepparent who is handling most of the conveniences in that child's life, this situation needs parenting. Not only will you need to parent the situation but your spouse will also need to unequivocally back you up by assisting you in the follow-through of your parenting decisions. If this assistance doesn't happen, you will not be able to parent. Therefore, you will not be able to continue handling the extra responsibilities of the stepchild in the home.

In that event, you must step away from parenting all together. You cannot parent a stepchild who knows you are not fully supported by their biological parent. Excusing yourself from the role of parent will be hard, and it will result in your spouse having to do much more for the child. I assure you, when your spouse is faced with the choice of helping enforce your parenting or having to do it all themself, your spouse will back you up. Your spouse will have no problem telling their child to pull their shit together and quit talking back when their Saturday morning tee time is threatened. Guaranteed.

My child and spouse aren't getting along. What should I do?

Breathe. This situation can cause the most strain on you, your marriage, and the children involved. We have all been through it. Biological child gets caught doing something stupid, is failing in school, breaks something, gets a speeding ticket, wrecks a car, costs the family money, what have you, and a stepparent's resentment to the situation cannot be squelched. Of course, as biological parents we are equally angry at our children when they do stupid shit, but we also see them as the whole child they are. We see where our shitty parenting influenced their bad decisions, we see where loss or tragedy in their life has changed them, and we see enough of their good to forgive their bad. A stepparent most likely does not. A stepparent gets stuck in the situation and the consequences. A biological parent can forgive more easily, but a stepparent may have a harder time letting go of anger or resentment.

So, what should you do? It depends. If the tension is a result of a failed test grade, don't do anything. Let the spouse be irritated and move on in a couple of days. If it is a more dire event such as a speeding ticket that increases insurance bills or brings trouble with the law, the fractured relationship will have to be addressed or the energy in the home will become unbearable for everyone.

We once saw a family counselor when my son was a young teen to help us through this exact question. One thing she taught us was to avoid the triangles in the relationships—we had to allow only two-way communication without creating a triangle, meaning that biological parents need to let the other two work it out on their own, and a stepparent needs to let a biological parent handle a situation as they see fit. A biological parent cannot give a consequence only to have the stepparent try to change it, and the biological parent cannot run to the defense of their child if a stepparent is unhappy with something the child has done. In a two-way conversation, no one is speaking for anyone else. Each person has their own voice, and only the two parties involved are in the conversation. Now, will they have the conversations on their own without the prodding of someone else? Maybe not. But in that case, you are now having a two-way conversation separately with each of them, asking them to listen to the other. You may not be able to have the conversation on their behalf, but you can ask them to go have lunch together, or take your car to the car wash together, or run an errand with each other. By avoiding triangular conversations, you can be the support instead of the participant.

My stepchild won't do their chores regularly without a battle. What should I do?

If your stepchild hasn't done their chores, rather than saying to your spouse, "Your kid didn't do his chores today," say to the child, "Go do your chores." If that doesn't work, then go to your spouse and say, "I just reminded Johnny to do his chores today. Can you please follow up to make sure they are completed?" If they are not, let it go. You did your part to move the situation along and it didn't work, so step aside. Instead of calling your spouse into the room, calling out your stepchild in front of everyone, and turning your kitchen into a combat zone, attempt to handle the situation with a simple reminder. If that is not respected, call in your spouse to back you up and confirm the chores get done. If that is not respected, odds are it's not going to change, and you will only make yourself crazy expecting it to. The sooner you make peace with it, the better your marriage will be.

I did everything you said, and the chores are still not getting done, which is creating more work for me. What should I do?

If you are doing more than your share of the household work because your stepchild does not routinely contribute to the running of the home, odds are you are getting angrier and angrier. Do not give yourself a brain aneurysm when discovering yet another child-created mess left behind for you to clean up. At this point, you have done everything you can. Don't continue to ask the child to do the chores but do ask your spouse to do them. Rather than recreating the cycle of conflict by asking a stepchild to do chores only to be ignored and then having to do the chores yourself, those chores are now your spouse's responsibility. If your spouse doesn't see a need for the stepchild to do the chores, and it's certainly not on you to do more work than you already are, then those chores have just become your spouse's responsibility. Whether it is taking out the trash, wiping down the counters, scrubbing toilets, or putting up dishes, if your stepchild is not expected to do it, then your spouse is agreeing to do it on their behalf. Either way, you are not taking on more than your share of the household work.

My stepchild's clothes never come back to our house. What should I do?

It depends. If you can afford it, buy more. Seriously, just buy more clothes. Especially when the child is young and a pair of shorts at Walmart costs only $3.99, buy four of them. Buy ten of them if you like. If you have the resources to stock up on extra clothing, just do it. It's not spoiling your stepchild or giving them too much, it is helping everyone keep their sanity by avoiding fights and saving the kid from being put in the middle of them. My daughter still wears some of her sister's old clothes that have DJ written on the inside for "Dad/Jamie" so we knew they came from our house. While clothing in a blended family is no laughing matter and causes actual strife for the children and the adults, I chuckle every time I see those old shirts because we were so petty and stupid. When you have young children, under ten especially, please do not ever expect them to remember to bring their clothes back home. It's unrealistic, and quite frankly, it's not the kids' fault they have two homes at such a young age. Cut them (and the parent in the other home) some slack because let's be honest: At 6:45 on a weekday morning, getting out of the house on time for a family with young children is a fucking feat in and of itself. Add to that the expectation to remember to put together a bag of clothes for the other parent's house, well, that's a breeding ground for conflict. At this very moment I have a bag of clothes with tags on them that I need to return to Old Navy to get my money back, and I haven't been able to make it happen for the last six months. Clothing in a blended family is one of those things that becomes about everything other than the actual clothes themselves. Nice clothes are kept home, old ones are sent back, games are played, and the kids are stuck in the middle while just trying to get dressed for school in the morning.

If you can't afford to buy extra clothes, the onus falls on you. Ask the ex to bag up some clothes and leave them on the porch for you to pick up. Plan a weekly clothing pickup on the same day you get the kids back. Make it a routine, but do not let arguments ensue, and don't let the kids get caught in the crossfire. When the text reminder is ignored, or the bag is not left out for pickup, assume positive intent and try again. Maybe it has just been a tough week for them too. Maybe they are just absent-minded and forget shit all the time or can't stay organized to save their life. If you were married to them, you should know firsthand it's just a personality flaw and not necessarily personal. You have no idea what is happening in that other parent's life, and it is not necessarily the slap in your face you may be perceiving it to be.

Another tip: Locate a resale shop in a rich neighborhood to stock up.

My stepchildren always forget stuff at their other house. What should I do?

It depends. By always, do you mean once a month? Once a week? Once a day? As stepparents, we can sometimes overstate how frequently our stepchildren are being irresponsible. If we have to go out of our way for them every so often, we translate that in our head as "all the time." Assess the situation honestly. How often is it happening, and why? If it is truly happening all the time, and by my standards this would be a weekly occurrence, some natural consequences will have to occur in order to create a greater level of responsibility for your stepchildren, especially teenagers. Older children cannot grow up expecting to be saved every time they forget a lunch, a uniform, or their favorite pair of jeans. The most obvious answer is that you should not go back to pick it up. Don't argue with them when they get shitty about it, and don't engage when they talk back. Just don't go pick it up. If it's important enough to them, they will get better at remembering.

If your spouse is the one taking the brunt of circling back, then let them do it. That's on them, and if they don't mind, then it's really none of your business, and this is where knowing the *why* comes into play. Maybe it is the only twenty-five minutes of the weekend your spouse and their kid will have time alone. Maybe they miss each other, and they enjoy having an excuse to turn around, stop for a drink on the way back or a quick bite to eat. If you are not the one being affected by an older stepchild forgetting items at the other parent's house, then quite frankly, who cares? Again, this may not be about responsibility or teaching a lesson. There is also a chance your frustration comes more from you, or your spouse, having to go to that other parent's house. Perhaps having to interact, or maybe just being in the driveway, makes your stomach churn and your anxiety levels increase. That's for you to work out, but it has nothing to do with the child involved.

Our other children at home are resentful for the double standards shown to my stepchildren. What should I do?

Again, it depends. How old are they? How often are the other children home? Is it an "our baby" or a stepchild? Children who have two homes tend to have more behavior issues, which does not mean they are bad kids, that the other parent is a bad parent, or that the other house lets them do whatever they want. Children with two homes grow up in two worlds. Two sets of standards. Two ways of doing things. Two sets of beliefs. Two religions. Two weekend routines. Two diets. Everything in their two lives is generally diametrically opposed to each other, hence the two homes in the first place. And don't forget to toss in the parent guilt that exists when a parent misses out on half their child's life. Because of these reasons, and so many more, double standards for stepchildren exist. There is no way around it, and that's okay, to some extent.

Stepchildren will likely be allowed to get away with more, whether it's not having to clean their rooms or do their own laundry or pick up after themselves or being corrected for talking back. When children have two homes, they are more confused. Their parents are trying to make up for lost time, and boundaries and expectations usually suffer.

So, what do we do when our biological children become resentful about having to do more around the house, or for having harsher consequences when they act out, or for the fact that they get less attention when the stepchildren are home? All very fair questions from the viewpoint of a child being held to a higher standard. The answer is that you talk to them. More importantly, you listen when they talk to you. You validate their feelings, and you acknowledge that it is not fair. Hopefully, you take something you have learned in this book and help them understand how their family is different. You explain that being different means having different problems than other families. You create empathy for the stepchildren going back and forth between homes. You help them understand it is not for a lack of love in the least. You hear them. You hold space. If they are at the point where they are noticing the double standard, then it's likely real, and their questioning of it is fair. They will learn that sometimes things aren't fair, and you can coach them through how to handle that new truth. You will need to have these conversations regularly. It will not be a one-and-done talk. It needs to become an ongoing conversation so that when they are frustrated about a specific scenario, they can talk to you. If you can make it better for them, great. If you cannot make it better, then you can help them process their feelings about it.

THE BLENDED MANIFESTO

Every situation, no matter how trivial or familiar, will test you differently. What matters most is the openness you approach it with and the understanding and compassion you choose to give to it. Trust me, your children are watching.

A Love Letter to Blending Couples

Dear Blending Lovers,

I see you. I know how hard y'all are working. I know how hard it is to make it all work. Don't give up. Get help, but don't give up. Our world needs your family to succeed. Your children, as angry as they may seem, need your family to succeed. You need your family to succeed. On dark days, cling to the moment you first saw your partner and those beginning moments of love—a love that likely found you when you needed it most, a love that walked into your life and declared a new direction for you all. Cling to that love like the life raft it is. You have likely had past lives and hurts and are probably still carrying around some of those bruises and scars. But this love, this love that created your family, it can defy all the rest. This love accepted you where you were and with what you had, children and all.

So, when it gets hard, and dear Lord Baby Jesus it will get hard, cling to that very first memory where it all began. Remember the minute love walked in and said, "I'll take it from here." Remember that night you drank a little too much wine, ate a little too much sushi, confessed a little too much to each other, and vowed to make a home out of all the combined crazy. Those people are still there. They get angry and hurt and resentful, and they often feel like they are doing everything wrong. But they are still there, and they still want each other. They just need a whole lot more forgiveness, understanding, and kindness than maybe either of you bargained for, maybe even when it feels like they do not deserve it.

Life in your blend can feel like the world is out to get you, like if it is this hard, maybe it just wasn't meant to be. Sadly, there is that reality, but I'm speaking to the ones who just need more work—the loves that still have a flame but are suffocated a bit from the stresses only blended families understand. I'm speaking to the lovers who just need a little oxygen to make it above water to the fresh air, the partners who go to bed angry but still find an ankle to hold throughout the night. You are my people. We are in the same fight. It's a fight worth showing up for, but it is as much about training as it is showing up on fight day.

Your family's success depends on our own inner work. We can't survive the blending if we don't retrain our hearts and minds or take the time to understand ourselves and each other and the battle scars we carry. We may have found a love willing to show up and step in, but we can lose it just as quickly if we aren't checking in with ourselves and each other. Frequently. If mental preparation is half the battle, and we aren't handling our mental health, then we are only working at a 50 percent capacity, and that won't be strong enough for this fight. We won't be ready to show up for our families, our partners, or ourselves. It's overwhelming, no doubt, but wasn't life on your own equally as overwhelming, just in different ways? Even if you were doing it all on your own again, you would still need to be doing your own work. You would still need to be facing your own blind spots. It would be easier though, right? Only managing your own past instead of everyone else's. That's what you think now because you've forgotten the dreams you prayed for, the family you craved, and the home you desired. Well, you have it now, and it requires more work than anyone anticipated. Hard, challenging, introspective work to check your own biases, your own resentments, your own anger, and your own anxieties.

These kids involved, these beautiful and battered souls at the heart of our struggles, we promised them a family and now we must follow through. We introduced them, we moved them, we forced them to come along for the ride, and we can't very well tell them it was all a big mistake because we aren't willing to grow and learn and forgive. Who will they become? How will their own families look someday? They have already seen what a broken family looks like, and now they deserve to see what a home can be. They may not be able to tell you how much of their own heart and soul is riding on this home, they may not even be able to tie their shoes or remember deodorant for themselves, but if they could, if our children had the ability to clearly communicate a feeling, I think they would tell us that they need to see an example of how love looks. They would tell us that no matter how much they push back, they are rooting for this family too. They want to know unconditional love—a love that didn't have to be taken on, the kind of love that may have had a moment to disappear, perhaps many, but stayed and grew instead.

So many of us are feeling alone, anxious, and misunderstood. The truth is that we are all those things. We are lurking in the shadows at school events, sitting in outfields at little league games, and taking the back seats to avoid overstepping or being seen. We are in the trenches, busting our asses, showing up for the daily events and the special occasions, all while trying not to take up too much space or bring undue attention to ourselves. Fuck that. This is our family, and these are our children. We have something beautiful to offer this world. We cannot continue apologizing for our families because it took someone else's falling apart for ours to exist. We exist, and our families deserve to be seen and heard. Our families are a crucial component to the world's success. Put your families on display, and your love. Something brought you to this life, with these children, and this partner. Now make it your own. It's your family, after all.

END NOTES

1. "The High Failure Rate of Second and Third Marriages," Psychology Today. Retrieved March 17, 2021. https://www.psychologytoday.com/us/blog/the-intelligent-divorce/201202/the-high-failure-rate-second-and-third-marriages

2. "Today's Statement of Strength." The John Maxwell Team. Retrieved March 22, 2021. https://www.johnmaxwellteam.com/2020-brendon-burchard/

3. Whitney Cummings, in an interview with Andrew Huberman, *Whitney Cummings Good for You.* Podcast. September 2, 2020.

4. Wilcox, Leisse. *To Call Myself Beloved: A Story of Hope, Healing, and Coming Home.* Toronto: YGTMama Media Co., 2020.

ACKNOWLEDGMENTS

Thank you is one of those terms that never seems to do justice for how you feel, so as I say "thank you," please also know I mean: I love you, you have been instrumental in my life, and I would not be who I am without you.

Thank you to my family. My husband and all those kids who all believed in me, supported me, got excited with me, and were willing to let me put our life on display with hope that it helps someone else in this world.

Thank you to my mom for the lessons, the freedoms, the unconditional love, and the constant (if not undeserving) blind faith in me and everything I have ever attempted to accomplish.

Thank you to my best friend for the decades of late nights, contemplating life and all its complexities, and helping me form opinions and beliefs I did not even know I had yet.

Thank you to Deanna, for forgiving with me, opening up to me, and growing alongside me. I know these babies will be better for the relationship we have forged along the way.

Thank you to Sabrina, Tania, Christine, and Doris and everyone else at YGTMedia for serving as my doula as I birthed this brain baby into existence. It would not be if not for finding your team.

Thank you to Leisse, for literally pointing me in the right direction, handing me the resources and serving as my coach, all while pushing me to believe in what I have to offer the world.

Thank you to Desiree, for hearing me out, calling me out, and seeing me through the last two years of recreating myself, rewiring my brain, and getting closer to the woman I want to be.

YGTMedia Co. is a blended boutique publishing house for mission-driven humans. We help seasoned and emerging authors "birth their brain babies" through a supportive and collaborative approach. Specializing in narrative nonfiction and adult and children's empowerment books, we believe that words can change the world, and we intend to do so one book at a time.

 www.ygtmama.com/publishing

 @ygtmama.media.co

 @ygtmama.media.co

Published in Canada, for Global Distribution
by YGTMedia Co.
www.ygtmama.com/publishing
To order additional copies of this book:
publishing@ygtmama.com

Developmental Editing by Tania Jane Moraes-Vaz
Edited by Christine Stock
Book design by Doris Chung
Cover design by Michelle Fairbanks
ePub & Kindle editions by Ellie Silpa

Printed in North America